5-INGREDIENT CAMPING COOKBOOK

5-INGREDIENT
CAMPING
COOKBOOK

Easy, Flavorful Recipes for Eating Well
in the Great Outdoors

PAULINE REYNOLDS-NUTTALL
Illustration by Claire McCracken

ROCKRIDGE
PRESS

To my husband, Alma, and my three children: Brook, Niva, and Eli; and a special shout-out to my mom and dad, who have inspired my love for the outdoors and for food.

For general information on our other products and services or to obtain technical support, please contact our Customer Care Department within the United States at (866) 744-2665, or outside the United States at (510) 253-0500.

Rockridge Press publishes its books in a variety of electronic and print formats. Some content that appears in print may not be available in electronic books, and vice versa.

TRADEMARKS: Rockridge Press and the Rockridge Press logo are trademarks or registered trademarks of Callisto Media Inc. and/or its affiliates, in the United States and other countries, and may not be used without written permission. All other trademarks are the property of their respective owners. Rockridge Press is not associated with any product or vendor mentioned in this book.

Cover and Interior Designer: Jennifer Hsu
Art Producer: Sara Feinstein
Editor: Anne Lowrey
Production Editor: Andrew Yackira
Production Manager: Michael Kay

Illustration © 2021 Claire McCracken.
All other art used under license from Shutterstock.com.

ISBN: Print 978-1-64876-391-5
     eBook 978-1-64876-392-2
R0

CONTENTS

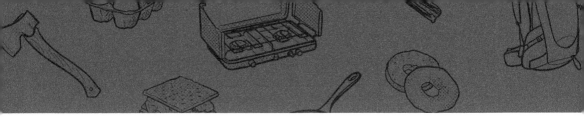

INTRODUCTION

Welcome to the wonderful world of camp cooking. I'm Pauline, the author of the *Cast-Iron Camping Cookbook* and owner-creator of *Mama Bear Outdoors*, an online blog and community that encourages people to get outside more. I'm so excited to share with you the art of cooking in the great outdoors. I am passionate about campfire cooking. Naturally, I'm usually the designated camp chef, and I enjoy every minute spent creating delicious meals and tasty treats for those with me.

On average, my family camps about 45 nights a year. That includes car camping, backpacking, and staying in our camping trailer. We see the outdoors as our playground, and we love experiencing new adventures wherever we go. As a family, we seek out new campgrounds and new camp meals for the fun of it.

The best camping trips involve creating fun memories around delicious food. Cooking outdoors can be tricky without the conveniences of a stove, oven, and refrigerator. Ingredients are limited because of space and the lack of refrigeration. But wonderful meals can be made with just a few

components. The recipes in this book include only 5 ingredients or fewer, including some fun and refreshing adult drinks you can enjoy around the fire. In these pages, you'll come to learn that you don't have to sacrifice eating tasty food just because you are camping.

This cookbook is for those who want to enjoy the outdoors while also eating well. All of the recipes have been created for those who love car camping or RV camping. Many of these recipes are specific to backpacking but can be made at any campsite, and likewise, several recipes can easily be modified for your next backpacking trip. There are so many ways to cook food while camping, and most of them are covered in this book.

This cookbook has seven chapters, with a complete chapter dedicated to camping tips and tools, safety, and useful information about cooking outdoors. I have included recipes for breakfast, lunch, dinner, dessert, snacks, and cocktails. I can't wait for you to enjoy these recipes as much as I do. So, let's take off on our next adventure: making yummy food.

CHAPTER 1

5-INGREDIENT CAMPING

Before you head out on your camping trip, there are a few things you need to know. This helpful chapter will cover the basics of 5-ingredient camp cooking, different types of camping, safety tips, fire building, leaving no trace, and everything you need to know about cooking over a fire outdoors.

Easy Camping

Camping is a great way to de-stress, take an affordable vacation, enjoy the outdoors, and spend more time with family and friends. When you're away from home, you still want to enjoy good food. Cooking while camping should be quick and easy so you can relax in the wilderness. Your meals should be filling and delicious, with the best and freshest ingredients that camping allows.

I love to cook at home, but I enjoy it even more when I am outdoors. It gives me such a unique opportunity to express my love of food. If you love amazing meals, being out in the woods, and trying new things, then you'll love this cookbook. I want to show you how to have the best camping trip possible by making mealtime special. If you go backpacking, there are many recipes in this cookbook that are specific to backpacking and others that can be tweaked for out-of-the-way treks.

Only 5 Ingredients. Really!

Every recipe in this cookbook requires 5 ingredients or fewer to make tasty and flavorful meals. And I really do mean 5 ingredients—not counting oil, water, salt, and pepper, which are part of your basic camping pantry. As much as possible, the recipes in this cookbook use fresh ingredients. Before we get to the recipes, let's discuss camping in general and some practical tips.

Car and RV Camping

Car camping is when you basically pack everything into the car and sleep in a tent at some wonderful and scenic location. RV camping is when you sleep in a camper and have some modern conveniences. Both are very different ways of camping but are similar because camping is camping no matter where you go or how you get there. You still must eat, and when you're outdoors, you need to cook a bit differently than you would at home.

The recipes in this book focus on basic car camping but are also good for RV camping. RVs have many conveniences, such as running water, kitchen appliances, refrigeration, and power, but camping is about being able to unplug and disconnect from the modern world. Even though your RV or camper may have a stove or oven, sometimes it's easier to cook over a campfire, and sometimes it's even beneficial because cooking outside gives you more room and helps prevents smells from lingering inside.

With car camping, you're less limited in what you can cook than if you are backpacking. You can cook over a camp stove, use a grill, or cook meals many ways over the campfire. Campfire cooking should be as exciting and fun as the whole camping experience.

Cooking Equipment for Car and RV Camping

Whether you are car camping or camping in a RV, you will need the same cooking equipment. It's important to have all the essential kitchen tools, because you probably won't be able to find a spare skillet or knife in the woods. There are two ways to make sure that you have everything you need. The first is to keep a checklist of all your camp kitchen equipment. The second is to have a set of necessities designated specifically for your camping box or RV.

I have created two lists of what you need for camp cooking. The first is essential cookware and other necessary items that every camp kitchen should have. The second list consists of items that you do not need but are nice to have that make camp cooking easier.

Must-Haves

KITCHEN TOOLS AND COOKWARE

- ☐ kitchen knife
- ☐ two cutting boards (one for meat and one for veggies)
- ☐ vegetable peeler
- ☐ 1-cup measuring cup
- ☐ measuring spoons
- ☐ mixing bowl
- ☐ whisk
- ☐ can opener
- ☐ fire forks
- ☐ large pot
- ☐ Dutch oven

- ☐ cast-iron skillet
- ☐ pie iron(s)
- ☐ meat thermometer
- ☐ tongs
- ☐ strainer
- ☐ long-handled spatula
- ☐ slotted spoon
- ☐ ladle

- ☐ three serving spoons
- ☐ enamel or stainless-steel dishes
- ☐ eating utensils
- ☐ drinking cups
- ☐ enamel coffee pot, French press, or percolator
- ☐ bottle opener

CLEANUP

- ☐ aluminum foil
- ☐ zip-top bags
- ☐ dish soap
- ☐ dish rags
- ☐ paper towels

- ☐ large water jugs
- ☐ bins (for washing dishes)
- ☐ trash bags
- ☐ hand sanitizer

CAMPING ACCESSORIES AND TOOLS

- ☐ cooler
- ☐ fire-starting kit, including a lighter or matches and fire starters
- ☐ campfire grate
- ☐ leather gloves
- ☐ first-aid kit

- ☐ headlamp
- ☐ flashlight
- ☐ toilet paper
- ☐ animal-resistant containers or a bear bag hanging system
- ☐ shovel

Nice-to-Haves

- [ ] cooler light
- [ ] jars or plastic containers, like Tupperware (for leftovers)
- [ ] pizza cutter
- [ ] paracord
- [ ] tarp
- [ ] awning
- [ ] collapsible trash can
- [ ] foldable table
- [ ] citronella candles
- [ ] bug netting
- [ ] clothesline
- [ ] grill scrubber
- [ ] dish rack
- [ ] disposable gloves
- [ ] sanitizing wipes
- [ ] ax or hatchet
- [ ] bellows (for tending the fire)
- [ ] fire extinguisher

Your Portable Pantry: Staples for Car and RV Camping

Before every camping trip, I plan out our meals so I know what ingredients I need to bring along. I find it helpful to always have a few basic ingredients on hand. My basic camping pantry contains staples that have a long shelf life and don't need to be refrigerated. I have a designated pantry box that includes my camping staples and other basic food items, like bread, chips, buns, and snacks.

In your portable pantry, you should always include foods that are canned, dehydrated, or even freeze-dried. Even though these food items aren't fresh, they are usually made with a single ingredient and no additives. Having ingredients that do not require refrigeration is always practical when camping. Besides my pantry staples, I usually include items such as instant potatoes, cans of soup, and dehydrated or freeze-dried vegetables and fruits. For many of the recipes in this book, you can swap out fresh ingredients for common canned, dehydrated, or freeze-dried ones to save on cooler space.

The following basics should be included in your portable pantry:

- ☐ baking soda (for putting out grease fires, to relieve bug bites, and as an ingredient)
- ☐ condiments (ideally, single servings, such as packets of mayonnaise, ketchup, mustard, hot sauce, and soy sauce)
- ☐ olive oil
- ☐ salt, plain and seasoned
- ☐ pepper
- ☐ spices and seasoning mixes
- ☐ pasta
- ☐ rice
- ☐ pancake mix, like Bisquick
- ☐ powdered milk
- ☐ powdered eggs
- ☐ sugar
- ☐ coffee

I think Bisquick (or pancake mix) is underrated as an ingredient. It can be used as a base for crust, dough, biscuits, dumplings, pancakes, waffles, and even desserts. For spices, I recommend using high-quality options because they tend to have better flavor.

Cooking Outdoors

There are many ways to cook outside when you are car camping. Depending on things like fire restrictions, how many people you are feeding, and even how comfortable you feel cooking over a campfire, there are different methods to consider. You might enjoy cooking in a Dutch oven, but it may not be practical if you are feeding just two people. Meals cooked in aluminum foil make for easy cleanup, but if you can't have a campfire, you'll need to try something else instead.

In this section, I break down different camp cooking techniques. There are benefits for each approach and tips and tricks to do it well. This cookbook has recipes that use all these different methods, so you have many options to choose from when menu planning for your camping trip.

When my family and I go camping, we cook over the fire or on a camp stove. Camp stoves are practical when you do not want to cook over a campfire, if there is rain, or if it's just too hot to light a fire. I also like to use my camp stove for making quick meals or a pot of coffee. A campfire, on the other hand, doesn't require special fuel, is the center of the campsite, and provides more options. It's also much easier to cook for a crowd using the campfire versus a small camp stove.

Camp Stoves

Camp stoves are used by many people who go car camping. They are good to have if you don't—or can't—cook over a fire. They are a popular choice for several reasons. One strong advantage of cooking with a camp stove is that it is very portable. You can put one on almost any surface you like—your car's bumper, a table, or even a stump. Fuel or propane canisters are affordable, can be bought even at the grocery store, and don't require a lot of space. You can use regular pots and pans, a cast-iron skillet, or a griddle on a camp stove. (Unless you are backpacking, you will want to use a full-size camp stove instead of a backpacking stove.) It's important to note that most recipes that are meant for camping stoves can be adjusted for cooking over the fire.

There are a variety of camp stove brands, such as Coleman, Outbound, and Camp Chef. When choosing yours, look for one that is durable and uses a common brand of fuel cylinders. There are one- and two-burner camp stoves—I like having two burners so I can cook more food at once. The most common, popular, and practical camp stove is made by Coleman. Coleman is known for its durability and quality of products. I have a Coleman stove that is more than 50 years old.

When choosing a camp stove, look for one that has a windbreak. If you plan on using a camp stove, be sure to bring enough fuel cylinders. An 8-ounce cylinder will last for 2 to 3 hours. I like the bigger 16-ounce canisters and typically plan for six meals per canister.

Campfire Cooking

A campfire is very versatile. It keeps you warm, wards off bugs, and provides a gathering area for everyone. Best of all, you can cook over it. You want to build a campfire that is just the right size for cooking and to be safe while doing it.

Before you go on your camping trip, be sure you are aware of the regulations in your area. This includes whether or not fires are allowed and any limitations due to fire season or air quality. Most campgrounds and trailheads will post regulations at the entrance, but you should always contact your local forest service office for the most current policies.

Campfires should always be made in an approved and established fire ring. At most campsites, these are usually made of metal and have been placed by local authorities. Others are made with rocks, but the local forest service has left them because they are established already.

There are several reasons to use an approved fire ring. The first is that the ground contains a lot of plant matter. A fire should always be built on top of dirt, because otherwise fire can burn downward and underneath the surface. Unfortunately, in 2016, Montana campers built their own firepit in a wooded area. The fire traveled underground, causing 8,658 acres to burn and 16 homes and 49 outbuildings to be destroyed. The blaze cost more than $11 million to suppress.

The second reason is so that the fire is contained. The third reason is to reduce your impact on the area. Imagine if every person who went camping made a fire in a new place—it would make the scenery less beautiful and would cause more damage. The final reason is that making a campfire outside of an approved fire ring can be a finable offense or, if you are camping on federal land or in wilderness, a felony.

Once you've located your fire ring and checked conditions, you'll want to ensure that the area around the fire ring is clear of debris or organic fuel. Remove any gear or equipment within eight feet of where your fire will be. Clear out anything that's flammable or presents a tripping hazard. Stack your firewood away from where floating embers could reach it. Do not build a fire within 200 feet of a body of water, to prevent chemicals and debris from entering the water system.

Always keep extra water by the fire for suppression. A shovel is also helpful to have nearby, as you can use it to move branches or wood that has fallen out of the ring back into the fire or to dig dirt to throw on the fire to put it out. A shovel is also useful for removing aluminum foil packets or a heavy Dutch oven from the fire.

Before putting anything in it, clear the firepit of trash. After you have removed any garbage, the first step to building your fire is gathering dry wood, kindling, and tinder. Most campsites will have firewood already cut, but often you can use fallen branches and downed trees. Be sure to check with the camp host or posted signs for regulations regarding firewood. Never cut down live trees for firewood. Not only can it be illegal, but green wood does not burn well. Use wood that is dry, or seasoned.

There are several ways to build a campfire, but the most common fire-building techniques are the pyramid or cone method and the cabin method, both of which use twigs, tinder, kindling, and larger pieces of firewood. For both methods, place a small amount of tinder, like grass, moss, pine needles, or dry leaves, in the center of the firepit on top of small twigs. If you are using a fire starter, place it in the middle. Fire starters make lighting a fire easier and can be purchased or even made with common things you can find around the house. My favorite fire starters are UCO Sweetfire and Pull Start Fire (see Resources, page 172).

Kindling is small pieces of wood that are about a foot long and no wider than three inches. It is used to establish the fire so you can then add bigger pieces. For the cone method, arrange your kindling into a cone shape around your tinder. For the cabin method, place four pieces of your kindling in a 12-by-12-inch square. Using additional kindling, start building up your "walls" by placing perpendicular pieces of kindling on top, alternating until you have four to six layers.

Have your wood and extra kindling nearby to build up your fire. Then, light your tinder. Gently blow or fan the fire until your kindling ignites. Add more kindling, then bigger pieces of wood until your fire is burning well. The best way to keep a fire going is to "bank" the coals, or concentrate your coals and burning wood together by heaping them in a pile, which maintains the intensity and heat. Add wood as needed when the coals and embers start to dwindle.

When you are cooking over a campfire, you don't want a very high flame. The best practice is to cook your food once the fire has burned down and you are left with just coals. To test how hot your coals are, you can use the hand method. Take your hand and hold it about four inches above the coals. Count the number of seconds ("one Mississippi, two Mississippi") you can keep it there.

2 to 3 seconds = high heat

4 seconds = medium heat

more than 4 seconds = low heat

Cooking over a fire is not an exact science. It depends on how hot your fire is, what type of wood you are burning, and even the weather. Heat levels can vary greatly, as can cook times. For the recipes in this book, assume that cooking is generally done over medium heat unless otherwise specified. I have done my best to make cook times as accurate as possible in this cookbook, but they may vary a little bit for you.

When you are done with your fire, be sure to extinguish it. Remember, "put out" means dead out. To properly extinguish a fire, let it burn down until there are no more big pieces of firewood. Then, slowly pour water over the fire while stirring with a stick or shovel. Once there is no more steam or smoke, hold your hand over the fire to check for heat.

‖ CAMP SAFETY FOR EVERYONE ‖

Safety should be your priority on any camping or backpacking trip. When you are in the middle of nowhere, being prepared for an emergency is important. Here are a few tips and reminders to stay safe on your next adventure.

» **Secure Your Food**
Be smart with your food storage. Use animal-proof coolers and containers or, while backpacking, a bear bag hanging system.

» **Practice Campfire Safety**
Be responsible when lighting a fire. Follow local regulations and guidelines. Never leave a fire unattended, and always put your fire out completely.

» **Bring a First-Aid Kit**
A first-aid kit should always be red, the universal color for emergency and first aid. It also makes it easier to find. Every first-aid kit should have the basics for treating cuts, burns,

bleeding, scrapes, and sprains, and include Tylenol or acetaminophen, aspirin, and Benadryl or diphenhydramine.

» **Pack Water**
Always bring enough water. I suggest, even if you are car camping, that you also have a way to purify water. There are various methods for doing this, such as using gravity filters, pump filters, water purification tablets, and UV light.

» **In Case of Emergency, Stay Calm**
In any emergency, such as getting lost or needing medical attention, it's important to stop for a moment and take a breath. Assess the situation and come up with a plan. If you're able to, call or radio for help. Be prepared for any scenario before you go, and always let someone know where you're going.

Campfire Grate

A campfire grate is awesome for camping and can be used to cook food directly over the fire like on a grill. Many campsites with metal fire rings will already have them, but you can always bring your own. I recommend getting one that has legs that fold up for a stable cooking surface. You can clean your grate before or after use with a grill scrubber or an onion—slice an onion in half and stab it with a fork, then spray the cut end with oil and rub it over the grate while it's hot.

Aluminum Foil

One of the most common and practical ways to cook over a fire is in aluminum foil packets. Foil packets are easy to put together and can be assembled at home and kept in your cooler. You can cook them directly on the coals. The best part is that they make for very little mess and very easy cleanup.

Using Cast Iron: Skillet, Dutch Oven, Pie Iron, Griddle, and More

I love cast iron for camping. This cookbook uses various cast-iron cookware. I own a pie iron, a skillet, a Dutch oven, skewers, and a griddle all made of cast iron. This is where menu planning is important, because then you know what type of cookware you need to bring. I choose cast iron because it's durable and heat resistant, which makes it perfect for camping. Cooking in cast iron is healthier than cooking in regular nonstick pans, which usually have harmful chemicals in the nonstick coating. Cast iron cooks more evenly because of how it absorbs heat. It is affordable and, if taken care of, can last forever. My family has a cast-iron skillet in perfect condition that is a century old.

Taking care of your cast-iron cookware is important. You don't want it to be rusty, flaky, or bumpy. Cast iron should be seasoned, meaning it should have a shiny patina—a smooth layer on the surface that keeps it nonstick. For best cast-iron care, use dish soap very rarely. Rinse cast iron and dry it completely. Rub oil on it when it's not in use. Throw in those little silica bead packets (the ones you get when you buy things like shoes) when storing it to reduce moisture. If you don't have silica bead packets, you can also fill a saltshaker loosely with rice and place that inside.

To keep cast iron from sticking, it needs to be seasoned. Most cast iron comes preseasoned, but you can do it yourself by using high heat and oil that has a high smoke point, such as vegetable oil or canola oil. See the Resources section in the back of the book (page 172) for links on how to season your cast-iron pan.

SKILLET

Cast-iron skillets can be used to cook over a fire or a camp stove. A 12-inch skillet is the best size and does not require a lid. I usually just use the lid from my Dutch oven if I need one. Many different meals can be made with just a skillet. If you are using a skillet to cook over a campfire, place it on top of a grate.

DUTCH OVEN

A Dutch oven is very versatile. You can cook soup or casseroles and even bake desserts or bread in it. When choosing a Dutch oven, opt for one with legs for better and safer cooking. Place your Dutch oven directly on the coals in the campfire. Then place more coals on top of the Dutch oven for even heat. Use the hand method (see page 13) to determine if you need more or fewer coals.

PIE IRON

Imagine a panini press on a stick. A pie iron is great for making sandwiches and meals for one person. If you are buying a pie iron, make sure it is cast iron. These are also made from steel or aluminum, but cast iron is better because it's nonstick and retains heat.

METAL SKEWERS

You can also get cast-iron skewers. They are hard to find but are less likely to bend, and because cast iron holds heat, they also cook food from the center. If you cannot find cast-iron skewers, steel ones or soaked bamboo will work.

GRIDDLE

Cast-iron griddles are nice to have, especially for things like pancakes. Most cast-iron griddles are flat on one side and have a grill pattern on the other side.

‖ OPTIMIZING STORAGE SPACE ‖

One of the biggest difficulties with camping is having enough room for everything. Whether space is limited to a backpack, a car, or even an RV, here are a few tips to help maximize your storage capacity.

» **Minimize** – Pack only the basics and what you know you will need and will use. Also, try packing smaller items. A good example is a foldable shovel versus a full-size one. Instead of full-size camp chairs, try using camping stools or stadium chairs because they take up a third of the space.

» **Multipurpose** – Instead of packing multiple items, try finding products that have a variety of uses. Multi-tools combine multiple gadgets, such as a knife, screwdriver, and wine opener. I have a multi-tool that is also a hatchet and a hammer and has all the attachments that most multi-tools have. By opting for a multi-tool, you are packing only one item instead of several. Other examples include sporks, bowls only (instead of both bowls and plates), and combination hand warmer/battery pack/ flashlight gadgets. Take a multipurpose soap, like Green Goo, that can be used for washing dishes, hair, hands, and clothes instead of needing to pack separate products for each.

» **Reduce** – Instead of packing large bottles of condiments or personal care products, use smaller, travel-size versions. Use soap sheets instead of a bar or liquid soap.

» **Organize** – Everything should have a designated place. Plan to use totes, storage cubes, and even stuff sacks to keep things organized and reduce the amount of space that you need for all your camping gear.

Backpacking

My family loves backpacking almost as much as camping. The big difference between car camping and backpacking is that for the latter, you haul everything in a backpack. Your car will usually be a few miles away. Every piece of gear, including your tent and anything you need for cooking, is carried in on your back.

Some of the things you need to consider for backpacking are weight, space, practicality, and perishability. It is not feasible to carry a large camp stove, grill, or cooler when you are backpacking. Lighter is better. Don't bring what you don't need. Backpacks are very limited in space, and there is no refrigerator in the backcountry.

Backpackers usually eat a large breakfast, dinner, and snacks during the day to stay fueled. Because it's not practical to have perishable items and cooking resources are very limited, most backpackers eat dehydrated or freeze-dried meals. Most prepackaged backpacker meals contain a lot of sodium and lots of preservatives. They usually aren't very delicious.

I make all of our backpacking meals. These are meals that can be made in one pot. I do like to include things like packets (not cans) of chicken and tuna, summer sausage, jerky, hard cheeses, and some fruits and vegetables that don't need to be kept refrigerated. Fresh fruit tends to be heavy, so I keep it to a minimum or bring dehydrated fruit instead. Many meals require adding water, so having enough water or a way to purify water is important. There are many different types of water filters, but when a recipe calls for adding water, I will boil the water from a natural source if it is available. I let it boil for 1 to 2 minutes. If you are using this method, take into consideration that you will need more fuel and that you'll have to bring it in, so account for more weight in your backpack. Also note that water takes longer to boil at higher altitudes.

There are recipes in this cookbook that are specific to backpacking (look for the icon), but many of the other recipes can be adapted with dehydrated, packaged, or freeze-dried ingredients.

Cooking Equipment for Backpacking

Because you must be very mindful of how and what you pack, cooking equipment must be kept to a minimum. When you are considering what to bring, be sure that you have everything you need to cook. Meal planning is probably the best tool for this. Most backpacking meals are made with a small stove and one pot. There are cooking systems out there specifically for backpacking, like those from Jetboil, MSR, and Fire Maple, but you can do just as well with a pocket stove (literally, it fits in your pocket) and a light-weight backpacking pan.

I have compiled two lists for cooking while backpacking: what you need and what is nice to have. I do like having the extras, but I pack them only if I have the room and I am not over my weight limit. Remember, lighter is better when it comes to backpacking.

Must-Haves

- [ ] 1-liter pot with lid
- [ ] lightweight backpacking stove
- [ ] backpacking spatula
- [ ] spork
- [ ] camping cup
- [ ] pocketknife
- [ ] water bottle
- [ ] water purifier (such as a water filter or water purification tablets)
- [ ] single-use soap sheets
- [ ] 2 clean cloths
- [ ] hand sanitizer
- [ ] fuel canisters (an 8-ounce canister will last 2 to 3 hours)
- [ ] lighter or matches
- [ ] bear canister or bear bag hanging system

Nice-to-Haves

- [ ] chef's knife
- [ ] microfiber towel
- [ ] zip-top bags
- [ ] aluminum foil
- [ ] mini seasoning bottles or shakers
- [ ] silicone travel tubes

Staples for Backpacking

For any backpacking trip, you should plan on packing a few staples, depending on what you're going to make and whether you prepare the dry portion of your meals at home. It is important to be well stocked, as many backpacking meals share a lot of the same ingredients. Cooking while backpacking has become much easier because so many choices have become more widely available, like dehydrated foods and single servings of chicken and tuna. Here are some of the basic pantry items that you will use not only out on the trail but also to make these meals.

- ☐ oil (individual packets or a small amount inside of a silicone travel tube)
- ☐ salt
- ☐ pepper
- ☐ spices
- ☐ powdered milk
- ☐ powdered eggs
- ☐ dehydrated or single-serving packets of meat or other protein
- ☐ instant mashed potatoes or dehydrated hash browns
- ☐ instant rice
- ☐ pasta

Cooking Out of a Backpack

Because having a campfire in the backcountry isn't always practical, most backpackers make their meals in one pot on a camp stove. There are plenty of recipes in this cookbook to make your next backpacking trip successful—by giving you the ability to eat delicious meals in the backcountry, with minimal ingredients and equipment.

Remember, backpacker meals in this cookbook are labeled with a little backpack icon for quick reference. Many of the other recipes will provide a tip on how to turn them into backpacking meals.

‖ LEAVE NO TRACE ‖

When you are camping or backpacking, please practice the seven "Leave No Trace" principles, which help you preserve nature and reduce your footprint. These should be followed for any outdoor activity. You want to leave the wilderness pristine and beautiful for others and for future generations to enjoy.

It made me sad when my family would show up to a campsite and there was garbage everywhere. The easiest way to do your part is to carry a bag for trash. My kids have turned picking up refuse into their favorite camping game. They call it a treasure hunt, and the one who picks up the largest quantity or the most unique piece of trash gets a dollar.

1. Plan and prepare. Research restrictions or regulations in the area and check the weather.
2. Travel and camp on a durable surface. Avoid muddy areas to prevent ruts. Try using areas that have already been used by other people. Do not make new trails.
3. Dispose of waste properly. Pack it in and pack it out.

4. Leave what you find. Take a picture instead. Don't pick flowers or cut down live trees.
5. Minimize campfire impact. Follow campfire rules.
6. Respect wildlife. Don't feed or touch the animals. If you do, this usually will lead to the authorities needing to euthanize them.
7. Be considerate of others. Anyone who spends time outdoors is there to enjoy it.

About the Recipes

All the recipes in this cookbook have been made outdoors while camping or backpacking. Some of them have even been passed down from older generations, adjusted to require 5 ingredients or fewer but retain the same flavor. Several of the recipes include simple directions and shortcuts that you can do at home in order to save time at the campsite.

This book not only provides you with delicious recipes but also gives you camp cooking secrets. The tips at the end of each recipe offer helpful hints or suggestions, including optional ingredients, substitutions, and even camping hacks.

Every recipe is labeled for dietary considerations, including dairy-free, gluten-free, nut-free, soy-free, vegan, and vegetarian designations. Other labels indicate the use of only one pot or one pan and recipes that take 30 minutes or less.

All of the recipes also include icons to indicate the cooking method—on a camp stove, in a Dutch oven, over a campfire, and over coals—or if no cooking is required. There are also icons representing whether a recipe is backpacker-friendly.

 BACKPACKER-FRIENDLY

 CAMP STOVE

 DUTCH OVEN

 NO-COOK

 OVER A CAMPFIRE

 OVER COALS

frozen
waffles

bacon

shredded
cheddar cheese

eggs

WAFFLE SANDWICH

BREAKFAST

Waffle Sandwiches

PREP TIME: 10 minutes   **COOK TIME:** 20 minutes   **YIELD:** Serves 4

NUT-FREE, SOY-FREE, 30 MINUTES OR LESS

Waffles are one of the most underrated camping breakfasts. Defrosted frozen waffles can be stored in your cooler for 2 to 3 days. They are easy to heat up in a skillet over the fire or camp stove or by toasting them on a grate over the fire. This breakfast sandwich uses waffles to create a variation that is very filling and easy to eat, as it doesn't require plates.

8 slices bacon

4 eggs

Seasoned salt

2 tablespoons olive oil

1 cup shredded cheddar cheese

8 frozen waffles, defrosted

PREP AHEAD

I cook my bacon at home to save time at the campsite. You can do it in a pan, an air fryer, or even the microwave. Cook according to the directions on the package. Once you have drained the grease and let the bacon cool, put it in a plastic bag or container and store it in the cooler.

1.   Preheat a cast-iron skillet over the fire on a campfire grate or on a camp stove over low heat for about 10 minutes.

2. Once the skillet is hot, place the bacon in it. Cook on each side for 5 to 7 minutes, or until the bacon is crisped. Drain the grease and remove the bacon.

3. Meanwhile, in a small bowl, whisk together the eggs and seasoned salt.

4. Add the oil to the skillet and heat for 2 to 3 minutes.

5. Add the eggs, stirring frequently, until cooked through, then add the cheese.

6. Remove the scrambled eggs from the skillet and set aside.

7. Heat the waffles and bacon on the grate or in the skillet on the camp stove until they are warm. The waffles can be lightly toasted.

8. Divide the cheesy eggs and bacon between 4 waffles and top with the remaining 4 waffles. Serve hot.

VARIATION: Salsa or sour cream makes an excellent addition to these sandwiches. To make this vegetarian, omit the bacon.

Honey-Nut Overnight Oats

PREP TIME: 10 minutes, plus overnight to soak   **YIELD:** Serves 1

SOY-FREE, VEGETARIAN

This is one of the best backpacking breakfasts that makes for a good breakfast for any time no fires or camp stoves are allowed. You mix all your ingredients together and let them sit overnight. In the morning, you simply open your container and eat. Because of the nut butter and honey, this recipe makes for a high-energy breakfast that can be easily doubled or tripled if you're in a group.

1 cup instant oats

1 tablespoon powdered milk

Dash salt

¾ cup water

1 (1.13-ounce) single-serving package nut butter

1 (0.03-ounce) single-serving package honey, such as Nature Nate's brand

PREP AHEAD

Mix together the instant oats, powdered milk, and salt at home and seal in a plastic bag or container.

1. Put the oats, milk, and salt in a container.

2. Add the water, nut butter, and honey.

3. Stir well and cover.

4. Let the mixture sit overnight.

5. Open in the morning and enjoy.

VARIATION: This can also be warmed up in the morning over a camp stove. Many variations of this recipe can be made, so try the following: cranberry and almond butter, dates and walnut butter, coconut and peanut butter, or raisin and sunflower seed butter.

Sausage and Egg Pita Pockets

PREP TIME: 10 minutes   COOK TIME: 20 minutes   YIELD: Serves 4

ONE-PAN, NUT-FREE, SOY-FREE, 30 MINUTES OR LESS

I like breakfasts that need very little cleanup. For those busy mornings when you are hurrying to get on the trail, this is the perfect breakfast, because you can carry it with you and eat it along the way.

1 pound ground sausage	2 tablespoons olive oil
8 eggs	1 cup shredded cheddar cheese
Seasoned salt	4 pitas, cut in half

PREP AHEAD

I cook my sausage at home to save time at the campsite. Cook according to the directions on the package. Once you have drained the grease and let the sausage cool, put it in a plastic bag or container and store in the cooler.

1. Preheat a cast-iron skillet over the fire on a campfire grate or on a camp stove over low heat for about 10 minutes.

2. Put the sausage in the skillet. Cook for 10 to 12 minutes, using the side of a spatula to chop larger pieces of sausage into smaller pieces. Drain the grease and set the sausage aside in a bowl.

3. Meanwhile, in a small bowl, whisk together the eggs and seasoned salt.

4. Add the oil to the skillet and heat for 2 to 3 minutes.

5. Add the eggs, stirring frequently, until cooked through.

6. Stir the sausage into the eggs thoroughly, then add the cheese. Remove from the heat.

7. Divide the mixture evenly between the pita pockets.

8. Serve hot.

VARIATION: Spread cream cheese or mayonnaise into the pita pockets before adding the filling for some extra creaminess and flavor. To make this vegetarian, replace the sausage with hash browns.

Foil Packet Breakfast

PREP TIME: 10 minutes   **COOK TIME:** 20 minutes   **YIELD:** Serves 4

GLUTEN-FREE, NUT-FREE, SOY-FREE, 30 MINUTES OR LESS

Meat, eggs, and potatoes are a very common breakfast combination. Making them this way while camping means fewer dishes and less cleanup. This is a hearty breakfast that will keep you full for an action-packed day outside.

1 (16-ounce) package frozen hash browns, defrosted, or 2 (4.2-ounce) packages dehydrated hash browns (rehydrated according to the package instructions)

8 eggs

1 pound sausage links or patties

1 (4-ounce) can green chiles

Seasoned salt

3 tablespoons olive oil or cooking spray

1. In a large bowl, mix together the hash browns, eggs, sausage, green chiles, and seasoned salt. Tear 4 (2-foot) pieces of heavy-duty aluminum foil and grease each piece lightly with the oil.

2. Divide the mixture evenly between the aluminum foil pieces.

3. Roll up the packets and seal all the edges.

4. Set the packets lightly on the coals.

5. After 10 minutes, flip the packets over and cook for 10 more minutes. Depending on how hot the coals are, they may need a few minutes more (or less) to cook after you have flipped them.

6. Remove from the heat.

7. Let cool for a few minutes and then enjoy. You can eat this right out of the aluminum foil packet or scoop it onto a plate.

BACKPACKER TIP: When backpacking, you can use dehydrated hash browns, dehydrated bacon or sausage, and powdered eggs.

COOKING TIP: If you do not want to start a fire in the morning, cook this in a skillet on a camp stove instead.

INGREDIENT TIP: You can crack the eggs into a jar at home to save space and to prevent a mess in your cooler. One egg equals ¼ cup. For easy portioning, a standard jam jar will hold 4 eggs.

Breakfast Biscuits

PREP TIME: 10 minutes   **COOK TIME:** 15 minutes   **YIELD:** 12 biscuits

ONE-PAN, NUT-FREE, SOY-FREE, VEGETARIAN, 30 MINUTES OR LESS

Biscuits make an easy breakfast. This biscuit recipe is very versatile, and you can use another ingredient in place of the raisins to fit your taste. I recommend trying crumbled bacon, cheddar cheese, Italian seasoning, or chives for a more savory biscuit.

2¼ cups pancake mix
½ cup raisins or dried currants
⅔ cup milk

Dash salt
Butter, for serving

1. Line a Dutch oven with parchment paper or a Dutch oven liner.

2. In a bowl, combine the pancake mix, raisins, milk, and salt.

3. Drop 12 spoonfuls of the mixture into the prepared Dutch oven.

4. Cover the Dutch oven and set it on the coals. Put some coals on top of the lid.

5. Cook for 10 minutes, or until golden brown, rotating a quarter turn every 3 minutes.

6. After 10 minutes, check the biscuits. If needed, cook for a few more minutes.

7. Remove from the heat and serve warm with butter.

VARIATION: This recipe without the raisins or currants can be made into plain biscuits and served with gravy. You can also drop the mixture into soup for dumplings.

INGREDIENT TIP: If you do not have milk, mix ⅔ cup of water with 5 teaspoons of powdered milk as a substitute. Two tablespoons of powdered milk with 1 cup of water equals 1 cup of milk.

Camper's Breakfast Tacos

PREP TIME: 10 minutes   **COOK TIME:** 10 minutes   **YIELD:** Serves 4

ONE-PAN, NUT-FREE, SOY-FREE, VEGETARIAN, 30 MINUTES OR LESS

One of my friends made this while we were camping, and I loved it from the very first bite. The cotija cheese is what makes this breakfast taco so flavorful. The raw spinach adds a bit of crunch and brightens up the other flavors. You can add the spinach to the eggs while they are scrambling if you prefer it cooked.

6 eggs	8 corn tortillas
Salt	½ cup grated cotija cheese
Black pepper	1 cup green salsa
2 tablespoons olive oil	1 cup fresh spinach

1. Preheat a cast-iron skillet over the fire on a campfire grate or on a camp stove over low heat for about 10 minutes.

2. While the skillet is preheating, in a small bowl, whisk together the eggs, salt, and pepper.

3. Add the oil to the skillet and heat for 2 to 3 minutes.

4. Add the eggs to the skillet, stirring frequently, until cooked through.

5. Remove the skillet from the heat.

6. Warm the tortillas over the fire on the grate or in the skillet on the camp stove for 30 to 40 seconds on each side.

7. Divide the eggs between the tortillas and top with equal amounts of cheese, salsa, and spinach.

8. Serve hot.

VARIATION: For additional flavor, try adding cilantro and/or bacon. You can also use hard taco shells instead of corn tortillas. Sour cream or green chile dip can also be added.

INGREDIENT TIP: You can use powdered eggs for this recipe. For 1 egg, mix 1 tablespoon of egg powder with 3 tablespoons of water and cook as you would for scrambled eggs.

15-Minute Hot Rice Cereal

PREP TIME: 5 minutes   **COOK TIME:** 5 minutes   **YIELD:** Serves 1

ONE-POT, NUT-FREE, SOY-FREE, VEGETARIAN, 30 MINUTES OR LESS

Rice pudding is more traditionally a dessert, but this has become one of my favorite backpacking breakfasts because it's fast, the ingredients don't weigh a lot, and there's no refrigeration required.

1 cup water

1 cup instant white rice

2 tablespoons powdered milk

1 tablespoon powdered egg

1 tablespoon raisins

½ teaspoon cinnamon

Sugar (optional)

PREP AHEAD

You can mix the rice, powdered milk, powdered egg, raisins, cinnamon, and sugar (if using) together at home. Store the mixture in a plastic bag or container. There's no refrigeration or cooler required.

1. In a pot on a camp stove over high heat, bring the water to a boil.

2. Add the rice, powdered milk, powdered egg, raisins, cinnamon, and sugar (if using), and reduce the burner to low heat.

3. Stir to combine and cook for 2 minutes.

4. Remove from the heat and serve hot.

VARIATION: Instead of raisins, try adding other dried fruit, such as cranberries, blueberries, or currants.

Apple Pie Dutch Baby

PREP TIME: 10 minutes   **COOK TIME:** 20 minutes   **YIELD:** Serves 4

ONE-PAN, NUT-FREE, SOY-FREE, VEGETARIAN, 30 MINUTES OR LESS

A Dutch baby (also known as a German pancake) is a very eggy, almost custard-like pancake. The butter gives the outside a flaky texture. I make this at home when we have something special to celebrate. The apple pie filling makes this easy and extra tasty.

8 tablespoons (1 stick) salted butter

6 eggs

1 cup milk

1 cup flour

1 (21-ounce) can apple pie filling

1. Cube the butter and place it in a Dutch oven.

2. Set the Dutch oven, uncovered, over the coals until the butter melts.

3. Meanwhile, in a bowl, beat the eggs lightly with the milk. Slowly add the flour, stirring, until combined.

4. Pour the batter over the melted butter in the Dutch oven. Spoon the apple pie filling onto the batter. Do not stir.

5. Put the lid on and place coals on top of the lid.

6. Cook for 20 minutes, rotating a quarter turn every 3 minutes.

7. Remove from the heat and serve hot.

VARIATION: You can make this without the apple pie filling and instead serve it with maple syrup, jam, or fresh berries.

Blueberry–Cream of Wheat Porridge

PREP TIME: 5 minutes   **COOK TIME:** 5 minutes   **YIELD:** Serves 1

ONE-POT, NUT-FREE, SOY-FREE, VEGETARIAN, 30 MINUTES OR LESS

Farina is an old-fashioned hot cereal that was created back in the late 1800s. The most popular brand is Cream of Wheat. It makes a very filling and quick camp breakfast–great for backpacking when you want something hot other than oatmeal. This recipe uses the instant Cream of Wheat brand, but you can use any instant farina.

1¼ cups water

¼ cup Cream of Wheat cereal or other farina

3 tablespoons powdered milk

2 tablespoons powdered butter

Pinch salt

1 teaspoon sugar (optional)

2 tablespoons blueberry jam

PREP AHEAD

You can mix together the cereal, powdered milk, powdered butter, salt, and sugar (if using) at home. Store in a plastic bag or container.

1. In a pot on a camp stove over high heat, heat the water until it is boiling.

2. Reduce the heat to medium and add the cereal, powdered milk, powdered butter, salt, and sugar (if using) while stirring.

3. Cook for an additional 2 to 3 minutes, stirring.

4. Remove from the heat. Stir in the blueberry jam and serve hot.

VARIATION: You can use any type of jam or even maple syrup for this recipe. Fresh berries or bananas can be substituted for the jam. If you do not have powdered butter, use 2 tablespoons of unsalted butter instead.

COOKING TIP: At higher altitudes, additional water may be needed. If the porridge looks dry, simply add some while cooking, a little at a time.

Breakfast Peppers

PREP TIME: 10 minutes   **COOK TIME:** 20 minutes   **YIELD:** Serves 4

GLUTEN-FREE, NUT-FREE, SOY-FREE, VEGETARIAN, 30 MINUTES OR LESS

Bell peppers taste great, and they tend to keep their freshness when stored in a cooler. This is a simple breakfast you can cook on mornings when you don't have a lot of time, like when you're packing up to go home. If you are making coffee, I recommend starting a fire beforehand so it's ready by the time you are done assembling the foil packets. You can use any color of bell pepper for this recipe; I like to use yellow bells because of their sweetness.

4 bell peppers

Seasoned salt

4 eggs

¾ cup shredded cheddar cheese

2 tablespoons olive oil

1. Rinse the peppers and cut the tops off, about ½ inch down. Remove the seeds.

2. Pat the peppers dry and sprinkle the insides with seasoned salt.

3. Crack 1 egg into each pepper.

4. Divide the cheese evenly between the peppers. Replace the pepper tops.

5. Tear 4 (12-inch) pieces of heavy-duty aluminum foil and lightly grease them with the oil.

6. Place a pepper in the center of each piece of foil, wrapping the foil around the pepper.

7. Place the foil packets directly onto hot coals. Cook for 10 minutes, flip the packets, then cook for 10 minutes more.

8. Remove from the heat and serve hot.

VARIATION: Add some chopped ham in the bottom of the peppers to create a deconstructed Denver omelet. If you prefer scrambled eggs, you can beat the eggs with a little milk and pour that into the peppers instead of cracking them.

Hiker's Breakfast Bread Bowls

PREP TIME: 10 minutes   **COOK TIME:** 20 minutes   **YIELD:** Serves 4

NUT-FREE, SOY-FREE, 30 MINUTES OR LESS

Eggs and toast are a classic breakfast, but when camping, you want a meal that doesn't use many dishes. And unless you have an RV, there's no toaster. If there is already a fire going when I wake up, this is what I cook.

4 round sandwich rolls

8 slices Canadian bacon

4 eggs

Seasoned salt

3 tablespoons olive oil or
   cooking spray

1. Cut the tops off the rolls, about ½ inch down.

2. Place 2 slices of Canadian bacon into each roll, lining the inside of the bread.

3. Crack 1 egg into each roll and sprinkle seasoned salt over the top. Gently replace the tops of the rolls.

4. Tear 4 (12-inch) pieces of heavy-duty aluminum foil and lightly grease them with the oil.

5. Place a roll in the center of each piece of foil, wrapping the foil around the roll.

6. Gently place the foil packets directly onto hot coals, cooking for 7 to 8 minutes on each side.

7. Remove from the heat and serve hot.

VARIATION: If you like eggs Benedict, serve these with Hollandaise sauce (which can be found in the gravy section at the grocery store). Heat the Hollandaise in a skillet on a camp stove according the package directions.

Philadelphia Roll Breakfast Bagels

PREP TIME: 10 minutes   YIELD: Serves 4
NUT-FREE, 30 MINUTES OR LESS

A hot breakfast is not always an option if there are fire restrictions or you are hurrying to clean up camp. Bagels make a good no-cook breakfast option. This variation has a great flavor combo and is more exciting than regular bagels and cream cheese.

4 ounces cream cheese

4 bagels, sliced

Salt

1 small cucumber, peeled and thinly sliced

2 (3.5-ounce) packages smoked salmon

Soy sauce, for serving

1. Spread the cream cheese evenly on the bagels.

2. Lightly salt the cucumber slices.

3. Arrange the salmon slices on each bagel half. Top with additional cucumber slices.

4. Add a dash of soy sauce to each and serve.

VARIATION: Use avocado instead of or in addition to the cucumber. You can also lightly toast the cut side of the bagels over the fire for 30 to 40 seconds.

sun-dried tomatoes

bell peppers

taco seasoning

hash browns

taco shell

VEGAN POTATO TACO

SANDWICHES AND SALADS

BLTS Sandwiches

PREP TIME: 10 minutes   **COOK TIME:** 15 minutes   **YIELD:** Serves 4

ONE-PAN, NUT-FREE, SOY-FREE, 30 MINUTES OR LESS

Not only is this an easy sandwich, but it is great to make on the last day of camping to use up any leftover fresh ingredients (which I usually have if we've made hamburgers). This sandwich is also a good choice for a hiking meal—I just add a packet of mayonnaise when I am ready to eat it on the trail.

8 slices bacon

4 sandwich rolls or hamburger buns, split

Condiments of your choice (optional)

8 slices Italian salami

1 tomato, thinly sliced

4 iceberg lettuce leaves

PREP AHEAD

You can cook the bacon ahead of time at home according to the instructions on the package. Drain the grease and cool. Store in a plastic bag or container in the cooler until ready to use.

1. Preheat a cast-iron skillet over the fire on a campfire grate or on a camp stove over low heat for about 10 minutes.

2. Once the skillet is hot, put the bacon in the skillet. Cook each side for 5 to 7 minutes or until the bacon is crisped. Drain the bacon grease.

3. Spread the rolls with condiments (if using).

4. Divide the salami, tomato, bacon, and lettuce between the rolls and serve.

INGREDIENT TIP: Instead of cooking the bacon at home or at the campsite, you can also buy it precooked at the grocery store.

Creamy Fruit Salad

PREP TIME: 5 minutes   **YIELD:** Serves 4

GLUTEN-FREE, NUT-FREE, SOY-FREE, VEGETARIAN, 30 MINUTES OR LESS

This fruit salad can be served as a side, a light breakfast, or lunch. I almost always pack the fruits used in this salad as a snack because they don't require refrigeration. This is a great recipe to make on the last day of camping to use up any leftover fruit so you don't have to take it home. This salad should not be made ahead of time because it gets a little brown and soggy if it sits for a while.

1 banana, sliced

1 apple, cored and cubed

1 orange, peeled and cubed

1 cup cubed watermelon

1 (5.3-ounce) container vanilla yogurt

1. In a medium bowl, mix together the banana, apple, orange, and watermelon.

2. Add the yogurt and mix well.

3. Serve immediately.

VARIATION: If you eat this for breakfast, try adding 1½ cups of muesli or granola. Any fruit can be substituted—use roughly 4 cups of fruit.

Camper's Chopped Salad

PREP TIME: 15 minutes   **YIELD:** Serves 4

ONE-POT, DAIRY-FREE, GLUTEN-FREE, NUT-FREE, SOY-FREE, VEGAN, 30 MINUTES OR LESS

This is one of the simplest salads to make. The ingredients store well without a cooler for a day or two, and I tend to make this when I am backpacking in a group because I can divide the weight between several backpacks. It can be eaten as is, as a side, in sandwiches, and can be made the day before without the tomatoes.

2 tomatoes	1 large lemon
2 cucumbers, peeled	1½ tablespoons olive oil
1 bell pepper	Salt
½ red onion	Black pepper

1. Chop the tomatoes, cucumbers, bell pepper, and onion. Place the chopped vegetables in a bowl.

2. Juice the lemon and add the lemon juice, olive oil, salt, and pepper to the vegetables.

3. Combine well and serve.

VARIATION: You can add feta cheese and sliced kalamata or black olives to make this into a Greek-inspired salad.

Backpacker Italian Pasta Salad

PREP TIME: 5 minutes   **COOK TIME:** 10 minutes   **YIELD:** Serves 1

ONE-POT, NUT-FREE, SOY-FREE, VEGETARIAN, 30 MINUTES OR LESS

This pasta salad is easy to prepare and none of the ingredients require refrigeration, so it makes for an easy and delicious backpacking meal. To make this for a group when car camping, simply quadruple the ingredients to serve four. This recipe uses the sun-dried tomatoes that are found in a packet, not the ones in a jar with oil.

2 cups water

½ teaspoon olive oil

Dash salt

1 cup penne or rotini

1 (1.2-ounce) single-serving package
 black or kalamata olives, sliced

3 tablespoons chopped
 sun-dried tomatoes

1 (1.5-ounce) single-serving package
 Italian dressing

1 teaspoon grated Parmesan cheese

1. In a pot on a camp stove over high heat, combine the water, oil, and salt. Bring it to a boil.

2. Add the pasta and cook for 7 to 8 minutes, or until al dente.

3. Remove from the heat and drain.

4. Rinse with cold water.

5. Add the olives, sun-dried tomatoes, Italian dressing, and Parmesan. Stir well and enjoy.

VARIATION: When car camping, you can add more ingredients, so try mixing in onions or feta cheese.

BACKPACKING TIP: Water may take longer to boil at higher altitudes. If you're backpacking and don't have a lot of water, you can skip rinsing the pasta even though it will take longer to cool and might be a little starchy.

Pie-Iron Pizza Pockets

PREP TIME: 10 minutes   **COOK TIME:** 20 minutes   **YIELD:** Serves 4

ONE-POT, NUT-FREE, SOY-FREE, VEGETARIAN, 30 MINUTES OR LESS

Pie irons are an easy way to use cast iron outdoors and make personal-size helpings. There are many things you can do with a pie iron, and one of my favorites is making pizza pockets. This is a quick way to make a hot grilled sandwich. Most pie irons have room for just one serving, so use 4 pie irons to cook 4 pizza pockets at the same time.

2 teaspoons olive oil

8 slices white or wheat bread

4 tablespoons marinara sauce

8 tablespoons shredded
  mozzarella cheese

1 teaspoon Italian seasoning

Pizza toppings of your
  choice (optional)

1. For each pizza pocket, grease a pie iron on both sides with the oil.

2. Place 1 slice of bread on the bottom.

3. Spread 1 tablespoon of marinara on the bread and add 2 tablespoons of cheese and ¼ teaspoon Italian seasoning. Add toppings of your choice (if using).

4. Put another slice of bread on top and close the pie iron.

5. Cook over medium heat just above the coals for 7 to 8 minutes on each side, or until the bread is toasted. It may take more or less time, depending on how close you have it to the fire and how hot the coals are.

6. Remove from the heat. Let cool for about 5 minutes before opening the pie iron.

7. Serve hot.

VARIATION: Try using different cheese and toppings in these sandwiches. Be creative with changing up the different flavors based on what you have on hand.

Vegan Potato Tacos

PREP TIME: 10 minutes   **COOK TIME:** 20 minutes   **YIELD:** Serves 4

ONE-POT, DAIRY-FREE, GLUTEN-FREE, NUT-FREE, SOY-FREE, VEGAN, 30 MINUTES OR LESS

These vegan tacos are so good that I promise you will not miss the meat. This is one of my favorite meatless meals. If you aren't vegan, feel free to add sour cream or cheese.

2 tablespoons olive oil

1 (1-pound) package diced
   hash browns

Salt

3 tablespoons taco seasoning

8 hard taco shells

2 bell peppers, seeded and julienned

1 cup chopped sun-dried tomatoes

PREP AHEAD

The peppers can be cut at home. Store in a plastic bag or container with a little bit of water.

1. Preheat a cast-iron skillet over the fire on a campfire grate or on a camp stove over low heat for 10 to 15 minutes.

2. Add the oil to the skillet and heat for 2 to 3 minutes.

3. Add the hash browns and cook for 8 to 12 minutes, or until golden brown.

4. Lightly salt the hash browns. Add the taco seasoning and mix thoroughly.

5. Cook for another 2 to 3 minutes. Remove from the heat.

6. Divide the potato mixture evenly between the taco shells.

7. Top each taco with peppers and sun-dried tomatoes.

8. Serve hot.

VARIATION: Additional toppings can be added for extra flavor and heat, such as salsa or sriracha.

BACKPACKING TIP: For 1 serving while backpacking, use 2 ounces of dehydrated hash browns, 2 tablespoons of dehydrated bell pepper, 1 to 2 teaspoons of taco seasoning, and 2 soft corn tortillas.

COOKING TIP: Make sure the oil is hot so that the hash browns crisp up quickly. If the oil is too cold, the potatoes will take longer to cook and will get mushy. You can also use 1 pound of fresh potatoes cut into ½-inch cubes instead of packaged hash browns.

Tuna Salad Lettuce Wraps

PREP TIME: 5 minutes   YIELD: Serves 4

DAIRY-FREE, GLUTEN-FREE, NUT-FREE, SOY-FREE, 30 MINUTES OR LESS

After a long hike, these tuna wraps have just the right amount of fiber and protein to help you regain your energy. It's also a fast and easy meal to make that's not too heavy. The only things that need to be kept cool are the eggs and lettuce.

2 (5-ounce) cans tuna, drained

1 (15-ounce) can sweet corn, drained

1 dill pickle, diced

3 hard-boiled eggs, diced

Salt

Black pepper

8 iceberg or romaine lettuce leaves

PREP AHEAD

Hard-boil the eggs at home for about 7 minutes in boiling water. Store them (with the shell on) in a container in your cooler until ready to use. The pickles can also be diced ahead of time.

1. In a medium bowl, mix the tuna, corn, pickle, and eggs until well combined. Add salt and pepper to taste.

2. Divide the tuna-egg mixture evenly between the lettuce leaves.

3. Roll each lettuce leaf like a burrito and serve.

68   5-INGREDIENT CAMPING COOKBOOK

Secret-Ingredient Coleslaw

PREP TIME: 15 minutes, plus 30 minutes to sit   **YIELD:** Serves 1

DAIRY-FREE, NUT-FREE, VEGETARIAN

Lemon is the special ingredient that makes this coleslaw so good. This coleslaw can be used as a side or even as a topping for sandwiches. You may want to make this coleslaw several hours before you eat it, or even the night before, because then it will be extra creamy.

5 tablespoons mayonnaise

Juice of 2 lemons (about ½ cup)

3 tablespoons sugar

Salt

3 cups shredded cabbage

2 carrots, grated

PREP AHEAD

The cabbage and carrots can be grated at home or bought preshredded. Store with a little bit of water to keep them fresh.

1. In a medium bowl, mix together the mayonnaise, lemon juice, sugar, and salt.

2. Add the cabbage and carrots and mix well.

3. Let sit at least 30 minutes before serving.

Easy BBQ Chicken Sliders

PREP TIME: 5 minutes   COOK TIME: 15 minutes   YIELD: Serves 4

ONE-POT, NUT-FREE, 30 MINUTES OR LESS

Barbecue pork or chicken sandwiches are a good way to feed a crowd. But slow-cooking meat over the fire would take all day. With this variation, you can make a hot slider in fewer than 30 minutes, and nobody can tell that the chicken came out of a can. This is a nice lunch or snack to make when it's raining because it is warm and comforting.

2 (12-ounce) cans chicken breast

1 cup barbecue sauce

1 (12-pack) sweet dinner rolls (such as Hawaiian rolls)

1 small red onion, thinly sliced

2 dill pickles, sliced

PREP AHEAD

The onion and pickles can be sliced at home and stored in a plastic bag or container in the cooler.

1. In a pot on a camp stove, combine the chicken and barbecue sauce. Cook over medium heat until heated through, stirring as needed. Make sure you break down the bigger chunks of chicken so they absorb the sauce.

2. Remove from the heat. Divide evenly between the 12 rolls.

3. Top with the onion and pickles.

4. Serve warm.

VARIATION: If you have leftover Secret-Ingredient Coleslaw (page 69), it can be added to these sliders. This can also be made with dehydrated pulled pork, such as Meat Shredz brand.

BACKPACKING TIP: For 1 serving for backpacking, use 2 Hawaiian rolls, 2 (1-ounce) single-serving packets of barbecue sauce, and 2 (3-ounce) pouches of chicken breast.

Grilled Cheese and Tomato Sandwiches

PREP TIME: 5 minutes   **COOK TIME:** 20 minutes   **YIELD:** Serves 4

ONE-POT, NUT-FREE, VEGETARIAN, 30 MINUTES OR LESS

One of the best cheeses for camping is Laughing Cow, the triangle cheese that doesn't need to be refrigerated. It can be eaten as a snack or put on sandwiches. With these grilled cheese sandwiches, you don't have to worry about your cheese getting soggy in the cooler or accidentally melting in the sun. The creamy cheese makes these sandwiches exciting to eat. I use mayonnaise packets to get the toasted bread crispy, so I don't have to worry about needing cooler space like I would have to with butter. Use 4 pie irons to cook all 4 sandwiches at once.

8 slices bread

8 wedges Laughing Cow cheese,
   original flavor

½ red onion, thinly sliced

1 large tomato, thinly sliced

3 tablespoons mayonnaise

PREP AHEAD

The onion can be sliced at home and stored in the cooler.

1. For each sandwich, spread 1 slice of bread with 2 cheese wedges.

2. Add onion and tomato slices and top with another slice of bread.

3. Spread ¾ tablespoon of mayo on the outside of the bread and put the sandwich into a pie iron.

4. Cook above the coals for 7 to 8 minutes on each side, or until the bread is toasted. It may take more or less time, depending on how close the pie iron is and how hot the coals are.

5. Remove from the heat. Let cool for about 5 minutes before opening the pie iron.

6. Serve warm, while the cheese is still hot.

VARIATION: Add precooked bacon or bacon bits for a smoky flavor and more texture. Also, there are other flavors of Laughing Cow cheese that would be delicious in this sandwich.

BACKPACKING TIP: Because the cheese doesn't require refrigeration, it makes a good ingredient for backpacking.

Fried Spam Sandwiches

PREP TIME: 5 minutes   **COOK TIME:** 5 minutes   **YIELD:** Serves 4

ONE-PAN, NUT-FREE, 30 MINUTES OR LESS

I think that almost every camper (who eats meat) has at least one can of Spam in their camping box in case of emergency or to enjoy for breakfast. It also makes delicious sandwiches if it has been fried. Cooking the Spam gives it a crispy texture and enhances its smoky flavor.

1 (12-ounce) can Spam

1 teaspoon olive oil

4 tablespoons mayonnaise

4 sandwich rolls, split

1 large tomato, thinly sliced

4 slices cheddar cheese

1. Cut the Spam into even slices.

2. Warm a skillet on a camp stove over medium heat, then add the oil.

3. Once the oil is hot, add the Spam slices.

4. Cook the Spam for 1 to 2 minutes on each side, or until browned, and remove from the heat.

5. Spread the mayo onto the rolls. Divide the fried Spam, tomato, and cheese evenly between the rolls and serve.

VARIATION: Try grilling this in a pie iron for a variation of a grilled cheese sandwich.

COOKING TIP: The Spam can also be cooked on a campfire grate.

Spinach-Salami Wraps

PREP TIME: 5 minutes   YIELD: Serves 4

DAIRY-FREE, NUT-FREE, SOY-FREE, 30 MINUTES OR LESS

Any type of wrap is a good choice for lunch while camping. This wrap also stores well, so it's a good choice to take with you if you are going to be away from camp for a bit. Because no cooking is required, it makes a good option for lunch during fire season.

1 cup hummus

4 large tortilla wraps

12 slices salami

1 large tomato, thinly sliced

3 cups fresh spinach

Salt

Black pepper

1. Spread the hummus on the wraps.

2. Divide the salami slices, tomato slices, and spinach equally between the wraps.

3. Add salt and pepper to taste.

4. Roll each wrap like a burrito and serve.

VARIATION: To spice this up, add pepperoncini, jalapeños, or sriracha.

heavy cream

spaghetti
sauce

diced
yellow onion

frozen meatballs

spaghetti

"SPECIAL SAUCE" SPAGHETTI & MEATBALLS

CHAPTER 4

MAINS

Dutch Oven Tortellini Soup

PREP TIME: 10 minutes   **COOK TIME:** 20 minutes   **YIELD:** Serves 4

NUT-FREE, SOY-FREE, VEGETARIAN, 30 MINUTES OR LESS

Tortellini store well in the cooler for a few days, and with this recipe you can use fresh or frozen. If you choose to use frozen tortellini, put them in your cooler frozen. This will help keep your cooler cold, and the tortellini should be thawed by the time you need to use them.

2 tablespoons olive oil

15 garlic cloves

7 cups water

1 (20-ounce) package cheese tortellini

3 (10.75-ounce) cans condensed tomato soup

2 tablespoons chopped fresh basil

Salt

Black pepper

⅓ cup grated Parmesan cheese

1. Pour the oil into a Dutch oven and set it over the coals. Once the oil is hot, add the garlic.

2. Sauté the garlic for 2 to 3 minutes. You want it to have a bit of color but not be cooked all the way through.

3. Add the water, tortellini, tomato soup, and basil. Add salt and pepper to taste. Cover and cook for 10 to 15 minutes, stirring and rotating the Dutch oven every 3 minutes until the soup is cooked through.

4. Remove from the heat. Garnish with the Parmesan cheese and serve hot.

INGREDIENT TIP: This soup is especially good with a side of garlic bread. Spread garlic butter on thick slices of French bread and toast for 3 to 5 minutes over the fire.

Cheesy Summer Sausage Grits

PREP TIME: 5 minutes   **COOK TIME:** 10 minutes   **YIELD:** Serves 1

ONE-POT, GLUTEN-FREE, NUT-FREE, 30 MINUTES OR LESS

Grits (or polenta) are underrated as backpacking food. After a long day of hiking or on cooler evenings, they are perfect for a hot and fast meal. The summer sausage in this dish adds extra flavor, and the cheese crisps give it texture. This also makes a good hot breakfast.

1½ cups water

1 cup quick grits or polenta

1 tablespoon freeze-dried chopped chives

Salt

¼ cup cubed summer sausage

2 tablespoons chopped cheese crisps

PREP AHEAD

In a plastic bag or plastic container, combine the grits, chives, and salt.

1. In a pot on a camp stove over high heat, bring the water to a boil.

2. Add the grits and chives. Add salt to taste. Boil for 3 to 5 minutes, or until the mixture has thickened.

3. Remove from the heat and stir in the summer sausage and cheese crisps.

4. Cover for 2 to 3 minutes, or until the cheese melts. Serve warm.

VARIATION: You can replace the cheese crisps with shredded cheddar cheese and use bacon bits instead of summer sausage. To make this vegetarian, omit the meat.

Chicken and Spinach Potatoes

PREP TIME: 10 minutes   **COOK TIME:** 40 minutes   **YIELD:** Serves 4

ONE-POT, NUT-FREE

This is one of the most comforting dishes that I make. It is one of those meals that just fills your belly with warmth. The original recipe also included dumplings, and my grandma would make it quite often in the wintertime. Over the years I have changed it up for camp cooking, but it is still a yummy recipe to make in the cooler months.

4 large potatoes

2 tablespoons olive oil

2 tablespoons minced fresh garlic

1 large chicken breast, cubed

1 (16-ounce) package fresh spinach

2 (1.32-ounce) packages country gravy mix

2½ cups water

PREP AHEAD

You can bake the potatoes at home in the oven. The chicken can also be cooked at home, either in the oven or in an electric pressure cooker. Store the cooked chicken in a plastic bag or container in the cooler.

1. Wrap each potato in aluminum foil.

2. Gently set the wrapped potatoes on low coals so they can cook while you are making the gravy. Cook for 15 to 20 minutes, flip them over, then cook on the other side for 15 to 20 minutes, depending on how hot the coals are.

3. Meanwhile, pour the oil into a Dutch oven and set it over the coals, next to the potatoes. Once the oil is hot, add the garlic, chicken, and spinach. Sauté until the spinach has shrunk, 5 to 7 minutes.

4. In a small bowl, combine the gravy mix with the water and add it to the chicken mixture.

5. Cook until the gravy has thickened, stirring frequently. More water may need to be added for higher altitudes.

6. Remove from the heat.

7. Once the potatoes are done, cut them in half and transfer to dishes. Top with the chicken and gravy mixture. Serve hot.

VARIATION: This gravy can also be served over mashed potatoes, biscuits, or rice.

INGREDIENT TIP: Instead of cooking the chicken at home, save even more time by using rotisserie chicken.

Salsa Verde Hot Dog Bowls

PREP TIME: 5 minutes   **COOK TIME:** 15 minutes   **YIELD:** Serves 4

ONE-PAN, DAIRY-FREE, GLUTEN-FREE, NUT-FREE, SOY-FREE, 30 MINUTES OR LESS

Hot dogs are such an easy camping meal, but you can easily get sick of them if they are the only thing you ever cook. This unique twist on hot dogs is very simple but packed with a lot of flavor. I usually cook this on a camp stove, but you can also make it in a Dutch oven.

1 tablespoon olive oil

8 hot dogs, sliced

½ cup chopped yellow onion

2 cups salsa verde

2 (15-ounce) cans navy or great
  northern beans, drained

Salt

Black pepper

PREP AHEAD

At home, slice the hot dogs and chop the onion to save time at the campsite. Store in the cooler in plastic bags or containers.

1. In a pan on a camp stove over medium heat, heat the olive oil for 2 to 3 minutes, or until hot. Add the hot dogs and onion and sauté until the onion becomes translucent.

2. Add the salsa verde and beans. Add salt and pepper to taste. Reduce the heat to low and cook for 7 to 10 minutes, or until the mixture is heated through.

3. Serve hot.

VARIATION: Try topping your hot dog bowl with cheddar cheese, sour cream, or even sauerkraut. This can also be served over toasted hot dog buns.

Quinoa Pizza Bowls

PREP TIME: 10 minutes   COOK TIME: 30 minutes   YIELD: Serves 4

DAIRY-FREE, GLUTEN-FREE, NUT-FREE

Our family really enjoys this recipe. I sometimes make it with rice and serve it as a salad or side dish. You can use any type of grain or grain mix for this recipe, like white or brown rice or even couscous. This is one of those recipes that you can mix and match with the toppings, too.

4 cups water

2½ cups quinoa

8 ounces pepperoni, chopped

1 (6-ounce) can black olives, sliced

1 cup cherry tomatoes, halved

1 tablespoon Italian seasoning

1 tablespoon olive oil

Salt

Black pepper

PREP AHEAD

Chop the pepperoni, tomatoes, and olives at home. Store in plastic bags or containers in the cooler. If you are going to eat this dish cold, you can also cook the quinoa ahead of time according to the package directions.

1. In a pot on a camp stove over high heat, bring the water to a boil. Add the quinoa and simmer over medium heat until cooked through and no liquid remains, 20 to 30 minutes (depending on altitude). Remove from the heat and transfer the quinoa to a bowl.

2. Add the pepperoni, olives, tomatoes, Italian seasoning, and olive oil. Add salt and pepper to taste, and stir well.

3. Serve hot, warm, or cold.

VARIATION: Instead of olive oil and Italian seasoning, try Italian salad dressing. Get creative and try adding scallions, green olives, kalamata olives, green peppers, sun-dried tomatoes, mushrooms, and any type of cheese.

BACKPACKING TIP: For backpacking, this can be made as a single serving. Use the following adjusted amounts: ½ cup of quinoa, 1 cup of water, ¼ cup of sun-dried tomatoes, ½ teaspoon of olive oil, 1 teaspoon of Italian seasoning, and 1 (1.5-ounce) package of black olives.

Drowning Pork Chops

PREP TIME: 10 minutes   **COOK TIME:** 40 minutes   **YIELD:** Serves 4

ONE-POT, NUT-FREE

This is a good option for fall camping because it's so filling. I often make this on our last camping trip of the year, when the temperatures drop at night to below freezing. I prefer cooking pork dishes like this one the first or second night because it is hard to keep fresh meat cold if you are relying on a cooler and have no way to get more ice. This is especially yummy when served alongside Camper's Chopped Salad (page 61) or Secret-Ingredient Coleslaw (page 69).

1 tablespoon olive oil

4 (4- to 6-ounce) pork chops, about
 1 inch thick

1 cup water

1 yellow onion, thinly sliced

1 tablespoon minced fresh garlic

2 (10-ounce) cans cream of
 mushroom soup

Salt

Black pepper

1 cup panko bread crumbs

PREP AHEAD
The onion can be sliced at home and kept in a plastic bag or container in the cooler.

1. Pour the oil into a Dutch oven or cast-iron skillet and set it over the coals. Once the oil is hot, add the pork chops and sear each side for 4 to 5 minutes, or until golden brown.

2. Add the water, onion, garlic, and soup. Add salt and pepper to taste. Cover and cook for 15 minutes on low heat, rotating the Dutch oven every 5 minutes.

3. Remove the cover and stir. Sprinkle the bread crumbs on top but do not stir them in.

4. Cover and cook for an additional 10 to 15 minutes, or until the pork is cooked through and no longer pink in the middle and the panko is golden, rotating every 5 minutes.

5. Remove from the heat and let cool for about 10 minutes. Serve hot or warm.

VARIATION: Use Italian-seasoned bread crumbs instead of panko, or add 1 cup of sliced mushrooms for additional flavor and texture.

Seasoned Stuffing Bowl

PREP TIME: 10 minutes   **COOK TIME:** 10 minutes   **YIELD:** Serves 1

ONE-PAN, NUT-FREE, SOY-FREE, 30 MINUTES OR LESS

I try to make all of my backpacking recipes easy to prepare. There are many variations of this recipe on the internet, but this one is extra simple and more flavorful. It can easily be served with instant mashed potatoes and gravy to turn it into a larger meal.

1 cup water

1 (2.6-ounce) can chicken

¼ cup dried cranberries

1 cup instant stuffing mix, any flavor

1 tablespoon dehydrated onion

1 teaspoon chicken bouillon powder

Salt

Black pepper

PREP AHEAD

Mix the cranberries, stuffing mix, onion, and bouillon powder together at home and store in a plastic container or package.

1. In a pan on a camp stove over high heat, bring the water to a boil.

2. Stir in the chicken, cranberries, stuffing mix, dehydrated onion, and bouillon powder. Add salt and pepper to taste. Cook, stirring, for 2 to 3 minutes.

3. Remove from the heat and let sit, covered, for about 5 minutes. Serve hot.

VARIATION: If you are not backpacking, try adding sautéed celery and onion for a more robust flavor.

INGREDIENT TIP: This can easily be doubled, tripled, or quadrupled by multiplying ingredients by the desired number of servings.

Salsa Shakshuka

PREP TIME: 5 minutes   COOK TIME: 25 minutes   YIELD: Serves 4

ONE-POT, DAIRY-FREE, VEGETARIAN, 30 MINUTES OR LESS

Shakshuka is the first Israeli recipe I learned, on my first-ever camping trip in Israel while I was a teenager. Though my Hebrew was limited, my friend tried explaining to me what it was, but all I knew was that it was delicious. This is a quick way to make this very popular dish, which can be eaten for breakfast or dinner.

2 tablespoons olive oil

4 cups salsa

1 tablespoon ground cumin

1 tablespoon minced fresh garlic

Salt

Black pepper

8 eggs

4 pitas or 1 loaf crusty French
  bread, sliced

1. Pour the oil into a Dutch oven or cast-iron skillet and set it over medium coals. Once the oil is hot, add the salsa, cumin, and garlic. Add salt and pepper to taste.

2. Cook until the mixture is bubbling, stirring intermittently, for 8 to 10 minutes.

3. Move the Dutch oven to coals with lower heat. Crack the eggs on top of the salsa mixture, cover, and continue to cook for 8 to 10 minutes, or until the eggs are almost cooked through but the yolks are still runny.

4. Remove from the heat and keep covered for an additional 5 minutes.

5. Serve hot or warm alongside the bread for scooping.

VARIATION: For additional flavor, add some feta or goat cheese before serving.

INGREDIENT TIP: Leaving the yolks runny adds additional flavor, but the eggs can be cooked all the way through if you prefer.

Pesto-Parmesan Pearled Couscous

PREP TIME: 5 minutes   COOK TIME: 20 minutes   YIELD: Serves 1

ONE-PAN, VEGETARIAN, 30 MINUTES OR LESS

Pearled couscous, also known as Israeli couscous, is an ingredient that works well for backpacking meals because it doesn't require a lot of technique to cook. This recipe looks and sounds fancy, but it takes very little time and tastes delicious.

2 teaspoons olive oil

1 cup pearled couscous

2 tablespoons pine nuts

1 cup water

2 tablespoons pesto

1 tablespoon grated Parmesan cheese

Salt

Black pepper

---

1. In a pan on a camp stove, heat the olive oil over medium heat. When the oil is hot, add the couscous and pine nuts.

2. Cook, stirring frequently, until the couscous and pine nuts have gained a golden color.

3. Add the water and bring to a boil. Lower to a simmer for 8 minutes, then reduce the heat to low.

4. Add the pesto and Parmesan. Add salt and pepper to taste. Cook for an additional 8 to 10 minutes, or until there is no more moisture and the couscous is soft. Serve warm.

3-Ingredient Catch of the Day

PREP TIME: 10 minutes   **COOK TIME:** 15 minutes   **YIELD:** Serves 1

GLUTEN-FREE, NUT-FREE, 30 MINUTES OR LESS

Fishing and backpacking do go together, but always have a backup plan for food in case the fish aren't biting. This recipe works well for most freshwater fish. I use a whole trout in this recipe, but you can also use fillets. You can cook this fish directly on coals or on a grate.

2 tablespoons powdered or fresh butter

1 tablespoon lemon-pepper seasoning

3 tablespoons water

1 fresh trout, gutted

1. In a small bowl, mix together the butter, lemon pepper, and water.

2. Spread the mixture on the inside and outside of the trout.

3. Wrap the trout in a double layer of aluminum foil and seal the edges.

4. Set the fish lightly onto the coals. Cook for 5 to 7 minutes on each side. It may need more time depending on how hot your coals are. When cooked, the fish should be flaky and no longer translucent.

5. Remove from the heat and let cool for 5 minutes. Serve hot.

Dutch Oven Sausage Casserole

PREP TIME: 10 minutes   **COOK TIME:** 30 minutes   **YIELD:** Serves 4

GLUTEN-FREE, NUT-FREE

This is a casserole that I often make at home in the oven, but it also works well for camping. I will often double it to serve a crowd. If there are any leftovers, you can eat them the next morning for a hearty breakfast.

2 tablespoons olive oil

1 pound Italian sausage

2 celery stalks, chopped

1 cup chopped white onion

5 cups water

2½ cups instant rice

2 (10.5-ounce) cans gluten-free cream of mushroom soup

Salt

Black pepper

PREP AHEAD

You can cook the sausage at home according to the package directions. Let it cool and store in a plastic bag or container in the cooler. Chop the onion and celery at home and store in a plastic bag or container together with a little bit of water to keep them fresh.

1. Pour the oil into a Dutch oven and set it over the coals. Once the oil is hot, add the sausage, celery, and onion and sauté until the sausage is browned and the vegetables are translucent.

2. Add the water, rice, and soup. Add salt and pepper to taste. Cook, covered, for about 20 minutes, or until the rice is cooked through, rotating the Dutch oven a quarter turn every 5 minutes. At higher altitudes, you may need additional water.

3. Remove from the heat and serve hot.

VARIATION: For additional flavor and texture, add 1 cup of sliced mushrooms.

Teriyaki Tri-Tip

PREP TIME: 5 minutes   **COOK TIME:** 1 to 2 hours   **YIELD:** Serves 4

DAIRY-FREE, GLUTEN-FREE, NUT-FREE

My husband is known to cook his tri-tip on every camping trip. Anyone who goes camping with us knows they are in for a treat when he breaks out the campfire grate. Now I am going to share his secret with you: It is all about the sear. Once the meat is seared, cook it over low heat until it reaches the temperature that you want. So, you will need a meat thermometer for this recipe. The length of time it takes to cook depends on how hot your coals are and what level of doneness you prefer. I recommend cooking these to medium-rare.

1 (2-pound) tri-tip   1 cup teriyaki sauce
2 tablespoons olive oil

PREP AHEAD

The day before your camping trip, marinate the meat: Put the tri-tip, oil, and teriyaki sauce into a plastic bag or container. Store it in your cooler.

1. Set a campfire grate over the fire. Make sure there is high heat, even some flame. The tri-tip should be at room temperature. Set the tri-tip onto the grate, reserving the juices.

2. Sear the tri-tip for about 8 minutes on each side, so the outside has some color.

3. Move the grate and tri-tip to a part of the fire where there is lower heat. Pour half of the reserved juices slowly over the tri-tip to reduce the flame flaring up. (If there are not any extra juices, you can brush the tri-tip with melted butter or olive oil.) Cook over low heat for about 20 minutes.

4. Flip the tri-tip over, pour the remaining juices over it, and cook for an additional 20 minutes, or until the tri-tip is the desired temperature in the center.

5. Let cool for 10 minutes, slice, and serve.

COOKING TIP: Check the temperature in the thickest part of the meat. Rare is 125°F, medium-rare is 135°F, medium is 145°F, medium-well is 150°F, and well-done is 160°F.

BBQ Steak Skewers

PREP TIME: 10 minutes   COOK TIME: 20 minutes   YIELD: Serves 4

DAIRY-FREE, GLUTEN-FREE, NUT-FREE, 30 MINUTES OR LESS

This is a wonderful recipe for skewers. Cleanup is minimal, especially if you use bamboo skewers, because you can throw them into the fire once you're done. If you don't want to use skewers or don't have any, you can also cut the steak into strips or leave it whole and cook directly on a grate.

2 pounds steak (such as skirt steak or sirloin), cut into 1-inch cubes

1 cup gluten-free barbecue sauce

¼ cup gluten-free Worcestershire sauce

1 teaspoon seasoned salt

1 tablespoon olive oil

PREP AHEAD

Cube the steak at home. Marinate in a container or plastic bag the night before with the barbecue sauce, Worcestershire sauce, seasoned salt, and olive oil.

1. Divide the cubed steak into 8 portions and thread onto 8 skewers.

2. Place a campfire grate over the fire. Place the skewers on the grate and cook over medium heat, rotating every 5 to 7 minutes, until the meat

is cooked through. Cooking times may vary depending on the heat of your fire.

3. Remove the skewers from the heat and serve hot.

COOKING TIP: To test how hot your fire is, use the hand method. Take your hand and put it about 4 inches above the fire. Count the number of seconds you can hold your hand (one Mississippi, two Mississippi). If it's 2 to 3 seconds, you have high heat; 4 seconds is medium heat; and more than 4 seconds is low heat.

INGREDIENT TIP: When you buy your meat, ask the butcher to cut it up to save a prep step.

Spicy Fish Stew

PREP TIME: 10 minutes   **COOK TIME:** 40 minutes   **YIELD:** Serves 4

ONE-POT, DAIRY-FREE, GLUTEN-FREE, NUT-FREE

This Spicy Fish Stew is a play on a traditional spicy Moroccan dish called *chraime*. It is traditionally cooked on Fridays. Because fresh ingredients aren't always accessible while camping and cooler space is limited, I use canned tomatoes and peppers. This dish can be served with crusty French bread or over rice, if desired. Because it is fish, this is one of the meals I make on the first night of camping.

2 tablespoons olive oil

4 fish fillets, such as halibut or tilapia, cut into large chunks

3 (10-ounce) cans diced tomatoes with green chiles

1 teaspoon ground cayenne pepper or hot paprika

1 teaspoon ground red paprika

1 chicken bouillon cube

1 cup water

Salt

Black pepper

1. Pour the oil into a Dutch oven and set it over the coals. Once the oil is hot, add the fish, tomatoes with chiles, cayenne, paprika, bouillon, and water. Add salt and pepper to taste, and stir well.

2. Cover the Dutch oven and cook the stew over low heat, stirring and rotating every 5 to 7 minutes, for 30 to 40 minutes, or until the fish is cooked through and flaky.

3. Remove from the heat and serve hot.

VARIATION: Try adding fresh parsley as a garnish for additional flavor.

COOKING TIP: Heating the olive oil first before adding the fish keeps it from sticking to the bottom.

Creamy Hobo Dinners

PREP TIME: 10 minutes **COOK TIME:** 30 minutes **YIELD:** Serves 4

GLUTEN-FREE, NUT-FREE, SOY-FREE

"Hobo dinners" are basically aluminum foil meals consisting of meat and various vegetables, usually carrots and potatoes, and are popular at campouts and scouting events. The secret ingredient in this version is cream of mushroom soup—it solves the problem of the food drying out and helps the foil packets cook evenly.

2 tablespoons olive oil or
  cooking spray
2 large Yukon Gold potatoes, cubed
2 carrots, sliced
1 cup diced onion

1 pound ground Italian sausage
1 (10-ounce) can gluten-free cream of
  mushroom soup
Salt
Black pepper

PREP AHEAD

Chop the vegetables at home. Rinse the potatoes well in cold water and store in water in a container. The water will keep the potatoes from turning brown. You can also assemble the foil packets at home, but the potatoes may change in texture though not flavor. If you make your packets at home, keep your potatoes in ice-cold water for a few hours beforehand.

1. Tear 4 (2-foot) pieces of aluminum foil and grease them lightly with the oil.

2. Divide the potatoes, carrots, onion, and sausage into 4 equal portions and layer them onto each piece of aluminum foil in that order. Top each with one-quarter of the soup. Add salt and pepper to taste.

3. Roll up the aluminum foil packages and seal the edges.

4. Set the packets gently onto the coals.

5. Cook for 15 minutes, flip over the packets, then cook for another 15 minutes. Depending on how hot the coals are, you may need a few minutes more (or less) to cook the packets after you have flipped them.

6. Remove from the heat.

7. Let cool for a few minutes and then enjoy. You can eat this right out of the aluminum foil packets or scoop it onto plates.

VARIATION: For additional flavor, you can also add chopped celery and mushrooms.

COOKING TIP: Your hobo dinners are ready when the potatoes and carrots are cooked through. Just carefully open a packet after 30 minutes, and if needed, put it back on the fire.

Sweet Potato–Black Bean Packets

PREP TIME: 10 minutes   **COOK TIME:** 20 minutes   **YIELD:** Serves 4

DAIRY-FREE, GLUTEN-FREE, NUT-FREE, SOY-FREE, VEGAN, 30 MINUTES OR LESS

It's hard to find a good foil packet recipe for vegans. This is a winner that is based on my vegan chili I always make. If you like the flavors but don't want to make foil packets, you can cook this in a Dutch oven—just add 3 cups of vegetable stock along with the other ingredients.

2 tablespoons olive oil

2 large sweet potatoes, peeled and thinly sliced

1 white onion, sliced

2 tablespoons minced fresh garlic

1 cup sweet chili sauce

2 (15-ounce) cans black beans, drained

Salt

Black pepper

PREP AHEAD

You can slice the sweet potatoes at home. Rinse the sliced potatoes well in cold water and store in water in a container. You can also assemble the packets at home and store them in the cooler.

1. Tear 4 (2-foot) pieces of aluminum foil and grease them lightly with the oil.

2. Divide the sweet potatoes, onion, garlic, chili sauce, and black beans into 4 equal portions and layer them on each piece of foil in that order. Add salt and pepper as desired.

3. Roll up the foil packets and seal all the edges.

4. Set the packets gently onto the coals.

5. Cook for 10 minutes, flip over the packets, then cook for another 10 minutes. Depending on how hot the fire is, you may need a few minutes more (or less) to cook the packets after you have flipped them.

6. Remove from the heat.

7. Let cool for a few minutes and then enjoy. You can eat this right out of the foil packets or scoop it onto plates.

VARIATION: You can add cumin for additional flavor. I often top mine with avocado after it's cooked for more flavor and healthy fats.

INGREDIENT TIP: If prepping ahead, pop the sweet potatoes into the microwave for 1 minute after stabbing them with a fork. This will make them easier to cut and peel.

Easy Ramen Noodle Bowls

PREP TIME: 5 minutes   COOK TIME: 5 minutes   YIELD: Serves 4

ONE-POT, DAIRY-FREE, NUT-FREE, 30 MINUTES OR LESS

When my husband is looking for a quick campsite lunch, this is what he makes. It's usually after he's had a long morning cutting firewood or going for a strenuous hike. What's great about this recipe is that you can add pretty much any other veggies to change up the flavors.

4 cups water

2 (3-ounce) packages instant ramen, chicken flavor

1 (14.5-ounce) can green beans, drained

1 (15.25-ounce) can sweet corn, drained

2 (9.75-ounce) cans chicken, drained

2 tablespoons soy sauce

Salt

Black pepper

1. In a pot on a camp stove over high heat, bring the water to a boil.

2. Break up the ramen noodles into chunks and add them to the water.

3. Once the water has come back to a boil, add the green beans, corn, chicken, and soy sauce. Add salt and pepper to taste.

4. Cook for 3 to 4 minutes. Remove from the heat.

5.   Ladle into 4 bowls and enjoy hot, because the noodles tend to get soft and soggy if not eaten right away.

BACKPACKING TIP: For backpacking, to make about 2 servings, use 1 package of ramen, 1 cup of water, ½ cup of dehydrated veggies, 1 single-serving packet of soy sauce, and 1 (2.6-ounce) single-serving pouch of chicken.

INGREDIENT TIP: You can replace the flavoring in the ramen noodle packets with a more robust chicken bouillon for even more flavor. I often add sliced mushrooms, broccoli, and even bean sprouts.

"Special Sauce" Spaghetti and Meatballs

PREP TIME: 5 minutes   **COOK TIME:** 25 minutes   **YIELD:** Serves 4

ONE-POT, NUT-FREE, SOY-FREE, 30 MINUTES OR LESS

Spaghetti makes a great family meal for camping and is easy to feed a crowd. I love vodka sauce with it, but it takes at least a day to get it right because the sauce needs to be slow cooked. With a few shortcuts, this spaghetti dish is just as good, if not better. My kids call it "special sauce."

4 quarts water

2 teaspoons salt, plus more
  for seasoning

4 tablespoons olive oil, divided

1 (16-ounce) package spaghetti

1 yellow onion, diced

1 (26-ounce) package frozen
  meatballs, defrosted

1 (24-ounce) jar spaghetti sauce

1 cup heavy (whipping) cream

Black pepper

PREP AHEAD

You can cook the noodles at home according to the package instructions. Rinse well, cool, and store in a plastic container or bag in the cooler.

1. On a camp stove, bring the water to a rolling boil. Add the salt, 2 tablespoons of olive oil, and the spaghetti to the water.

2. Once the water has come back to a boil, cook uncovered for 10 to 12 minutes, stirring occasionally, until the spaghetti is done.

3. Drain the spaghetti and set aside.

4. Pour the remaining 2 tablespoons of oil into a Dutch oven and set it over the coals. Once the oil is hot, add the onion and meatballs and cook for 5 to 10 minutes, or until heated through.

5. Add the spaghetti, sauce, and heavy cream. Add salt and pepper to taste. Cook, stirring, until the sauce starts to bubble.

6. Remove from the heat and serve hot.

VARIATION: Top with Parmesan or serve with garlic bread. To make this vegetarian, omit the meatballs. For a more robust vegetarian sauce, add peppers and mushrooms.

INGREDIENT TIP: Depending on what jarred spaghetti sauce you use, you might want to add extra Italian seasoning or basil for flavor.

Bacon and Cheddar Potato Boats

PREP TIME: 10 minutes   **COOK TIME:** 40 minutes   **YIELD:** Serves 4

GLUTEN-FREE, NUT-FREE, SOY-FREE

The first "camping" food I learned to make was plain baked potatoes. You simply wash them, wrap them in foil, and put them in the coals until they are done. Looking back now, I don't know how I could eat just a potato, with nothing on it. These are my trusty elevated campfire-baked potatoes.

4 large russet potatoes

8 thick slices bacon, cut into quarters

4 slices cheddar cheese, cut
   into quarters

Salt

Black pepper

Sour cream (optional)

Scallions, white and green parts,
   chopped (optional)

1. Make 5 crosswise cuts in each potato, but do not slice all the way through.

2. In each cut, place a piece each of bacon and cheddar. Sprinkle with salt and pepper.

3. Tightly wrap each potato in a 12-inch piece of heavy-duty aluminum foil.

4. Gently set the wrapped potatoes onto the coals. Cook for 15 to 20 minutes, flip, then cook on the other side for another 15 to 20 minutes, or until the potato and bacon are cooked through. Cook times may vary depending on how hot your fire is.

5. Remove from the heat and let cool for about 5 minutes.

6. Top with a dollop of sour cream (if using) and a sprinkling of scallions (if using). Serve warm.

SERVING TIP: You can make these into a hearty breakfast by serving the potatoes with scrambled eggs. You can also top with fresh or freeze-dried chives and extra cheese for more flavor.

Campfire Mac & Cheese

PREP TIME: 10 minutes   **COOK TIME:** 35 minutes   **YIELD:** Serves 6

NUT-FREE, SOY-FREE, VEGETARIAN

One of my family's favorite camping meals is this mac and cheese. The best thing about it is that because it is cooked in aluminum foil packets, the cheese gets nice and crispy on the edges—which makes it extra decadent. Making this recipe is a good way to start cooking with foil packets because it is nearly foolproof.

2 tablespoons olive oil, divided

4 quarts water

2 teaspoons salt, plus more
  for seasoning

1 (16-ounce) package macaroni

1 cup milk

1½ cups shredded cheddar cheese

1 (24-ounce) jar Alfredo sauce

Black pepper

PREP AHEAD

You can cook the pasta at home according to the package directions. Rinse well and store in a container in your cooler until you are ready to make this recipe. The foil packets can also be assembled ahead of time at home and stored in the cooler, so that all you have to do at the campsite is cook them over the fire.

1. Tear 6 (2-foot) pieces of heavy-duty aluminum foil and grease each piece lightly with ¼ tablespoon of oil.

2. Pour the water into a large pot and place it on a camp stove. Add the salt and the remaining ½ tablespoon of oil to the water and bring to a rolling boil over high heat.

3. Add the macaroni and cook, stirring occasionally, for 10 to 12 minutes, or until al dente.

4. Remove from the heat and drain the pasta. Return the drained macaroni to the empty pot and stir in the milk, cheddar, and Alfredo sauce. Add salt and pepper to taste.

5. Divide the mixture equally between the prepared aluminum foil pieces.

6. Roll up the aluminum foil packets and seal the edges.

7. Set the packets gently onto the coals.

8. Cook for 10 minutes, flip over the packets, then cook on the other side for 10 more minutes. Depending on how hot the coals are, you may need a few minutes more (or less) to cook the packets after you have flipped them.

⟶

9. Remove from the heat.

10. Let cool for a few minutes and then enjoy. You can eat this right out of the aluminum foil packets or scoop it into bowls.

VARIATION: Add diced chicken, sliced hot dogs, Spam, or bacon bits to add protein and extra flavor.

BACKPACKING TIP: To adjust for backpacking and 1 portion, use 1 cup of dried pasta, 3 tablespoons of powdered milk, 3 tablespoons of grated Parmesan, salt, and pepper. Boil the pasta in 1½ cups of water on your stove until al dente, about 7 minutes, but do not drain. Add the dry ingredients and continue cooking until the sauce has thickened.

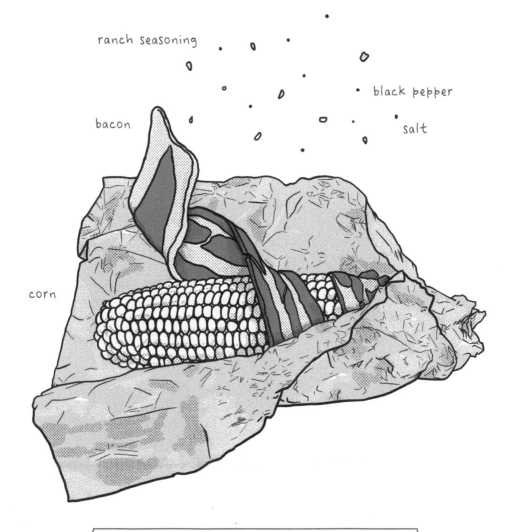

ranch seasoning

bacon

black pepper

salt

corn

BACON-RANCH CORN ON THE COB

CHAPTER 5

SNACKS AND SIDES

Peppered Beef Jerky

PREP TIME: 10 minutes, plus 1 to 2 hours to freeze and 24 hours to marinate

COOK TIME: 7 hours

YIELD: Serves 4

DAIRY-FREE, GLUTEN-FREE, NUT-FREE, SOY-FREE

Beef jerky is a good snack for any outdoor activity. I try to make my own at home every year, even though it is time-consuming, because I like to know what is in it and experiment with flavors. Also, it is usually cheaper to make than buy. When choosing meat for jerky, you want the least amount of fat. If you do not have a dehydrator, you can make jerky in the oven. Be sure to plan ahead as you'll be taking this with you rather than making it at the campsite.

1 pound lean beef (such as skirt steak or eye of round), trimmed of all fat

½ cup gluten-free Worcestershire sauce

2 teaspoons liquid smoke

3 tablespoons brown sugar or honey

1 tablespoon freshly ground black pepper

Salt

1. Freeze the beef for 1 to 2 hours. Take it out of the freezer and cut with the grain into thin slices. To save time, ask the butcher to slice your meat for you.

2. In a small bowl, whisk together the Worcestershire sauce, liquid smoke, brown sugar, pepper, and salt to taste. Transfer the marinade to a

container or zip-top bag and add the beef. Marinate for 24 hours in the refrigerator.

3. Set a dehydrator to 160°F. Lay the marinated beef onto the rack with adequate space in between each slice. Cook for 1 hour 30 minutes, rotate the racks, and cook for another 1 hour 30 minutes.

4. Reduce the temperature to 130°F. Again, rotate the racks. Cook for 2 hours. Rotate the racks and cook for another 2 hours.

5. At this point, the jerky should be close to done. It should be firm but bendable. If needed, rotate the racks again and continue to cook, checking the jerky every 30 minutes. Because the meat slices may not all have the same thickness, some might be done earlier than others.

6. Jerky will keep for 7 days in a container or bag. To store for longer, place in vacuum-packed bags and store in the freezer for up to 2 months.

VARIATION: Try adding other flavors, such as soy, garlic, and red pepper flakes.

COOKING TIP: Depending on your dehydrator, you might need to lightly grease the racks before you start your jerky. To make jerky in an oven, use the same temperatures and keep the oven slightly open. Not all ovens have temperatures this low, so use the lowest temperature setting. Lay the marinated beef slices on parchment-lined baking sheets and turn the meat over every 2 hours.

Strawberry Fruit Leather

PREP TIME: 10 minutes   **COOK TIME:** 4 to 6 hours   **YIELD:** Serves 4

DAIRY-FREE, GLUTEN-FREE, NUT-FREE, SOY-FREE, VEGAN

With only three ingredients, this is a much healthier version of fruit leather than what you can buy in the store. This recipe requires an oven or a dehydrator, so plan ahead to make it at home rather than on the road. I often triple the batch and store it in the freezer. Note that you do not have to use strawberries—you can use other fruits, such as plums, raspberries, peaches, and apricots. Strawberries, however, are available almost any time of the year. The cook time on this is variable, because it really depends on the dehydrating method you use.

4 cups strawberries, hulled   **¼ cup lemon juice**
½ cup sugar

1. In a blender, blend the strawberries, sugar, and lemon juice until smooth. Let sit for about 15 minutes, then strain out any seeds or lumps.

2. Set a dehydrator to 145°F. Line two racks with parchment paper. Spread the mixture as thin as possible. You may need an additional rack if the fruit is extra juicy.

3. Cook for 4 to 6 hours, rotating the racks every hour. After 4 hours, start checking to see if it is done. It should be soft but no longer tacky to the touch.

4. Store for up to 7 days in a plastic container or bag. Store for 1 to 2 months in a vacuum-sealed bag or in the freezer.

VARIATION: You can mix and match fruit. Try one of these combos: honey and peach, mixed berries, or strawberry and rhubarb.

COOKING TIP: To make this in an oven, line two baking sheets with parchment paper and spread them with the strawberry mixture. Bake at 140°F, leaving the oven open a crack and rotating every hour. In the oven, the fruit leather will sometimes get crispy at the edges.

Veggie Snack Platter

PREP TIME: 10 minutes   **YIELD:** Serves 4

GLUTEN-FREE, NUT-FREE, SOY-FREE, VEGETARIAN, 30 MINUTES OR LESS

Fresh veggies and dip make a great snack or even a side. This is one of my favorite things to keep on hand for snacking in between meals when we are camping. Not only is it healthy, but the whole thing can be prepped at home. Portion in covered containers and set in the cooler. When you are ready to eat, just take it out, arrange on a plate, and serve.

1 cup baby carrots	1 cup cauliflower florets
2 celery stalks, cut into quarters	1 cup ranch dressing or dip
1 cup broccoli florets	

1. Arrange the carrots, celery pieces, broccoli florets, and cauliflower florets on a plate.
2. Pour the ranch dressing into a small container and place in the center.
3. Serve.

VARIATION: I often make my own ranch dip using 1 cup of sour cream, 1 tablespoon of lemon juice, 3 tablespoons of water, ½ teaspoon of garlic salt, 1 teaspoon of dried dill, 1 teaspoon of dehydrated onion or chives, and 1 teaspoon of dried parsley. Other vegetables you can use include bell peppers, cucumbers, and sugar snap peas.

Meat and Cheese Board

PREP TIME: 10 minutes   **YIELD:** Serves 4

NUT-FREE, SOY-FREE, 30 MINUTES OR LESS

Imagine eating a fancy cheese and meat board around the campfire, like having a little picnic. Although you can use any combination of meats and cheeses, smoked meats and hard cheeses are excellent choices for camping because they do not necessarily need a cooler. The harder and drier the cheese, the longer it will last. Cheddar, Parmesan, Gouda, and Edam can last a few weeks. The key is to wrap cheese in parchment or brown paper, so it keeps longer. Do not cut the meat or cheese until you are ready to eat it, because it stays fresher that way.

1 (8-ounce) summer sausage

3 ounces pepperoni

8 ounces cheddar cheese

8 ounces Gouda cheese

1 (8-ounce) box crackers

1. Cut the summer sausage, pepperoni, cheddar, and Gouda into bite-size pieces and arrange on a plate.

2. Place the crackers in the center.

3. Serve immediately.

SERVING TIP: If you do not have a plate or tray, serve this on a clean rock or piece of wood instead.

Coconut Rice Crispy Bars

PREP TIME: 10 minutes, plus 1 to 2 hours to set   **COOK TIME:** 10 minutes   **YIELD:** 12 bars

GLUTEN-FREE

Cookies and bars make great snacks for when you are out hiking or backpacking and want something sweet and convenient. These rice crispy bars are perfect for being outdoors, and they keep well in your pack. Make them at home for an easy snack or sweet.

5 tablespoons salted butter, divided

1 (10-ounce) bag marshmallows

6½ cups cocoa rice cereal, such as Cocoa Krispies

¼ cup sweetened coconut

¼ cup chopped almonds

1. Grease a 9-by-13 baking dish with 1 tablespoon of butter.

2. In a large saucepan on a camp stove over medium heat, combine the remaining 4 tablespoons of butter and the marshmallows, stirring constantly, until the marshmallows are completely melted.

3. Remove from the heat and stir in the rice cereal, coconut, and almonds. Immediately pour the mixture into the prepared baking dish.

4. Let set 1 to 2 hours. Cut into 12 bars and store in an airtight container or individually wrap in plastic wrap.

VARIATION: To make these more like power bars, add ¼ cup of chocolate protein powder.

Bacon-Ranch Corn on the Cob

PREP TIME: 10 minutes   **COOK TIME:** 20 minutes   **YIELD:** Serves 4
GLUTEN-FREE, NUT-FREE, SOY-FREE, 30 MINUTES OR LESS

Like baked potatoes, corn on the cob is easy to cook over hot coals. This is the way we like to eat it, because the bacon adds so much flavor to the corn. This can be eaten as a snack, a side, or even a light dinner if you aren't very hungry.

4 ears sweet yellow corn, husked   Salt
1 (0.5-ounce) packet ranch seasoning   Black pepper
8 slices smoked bacon

1. Tear 4 (12-by-12-inch) pieces of heavy-duty aluminum foil.

2. Sprinkle the corn with the ranch seasoning. Wrap each ear of corn with 2 slices bacon so it is completely covered. Add salt and pepper as desired (usually, the bacon and ranch seasoning will add sufficient salt).

3. Wrap each ear of corn in a piece of foil and seal the edges.

4. Gently lay the foil packets on the coals. Cook for 10 minutes on each side. Depending on the heat of the coals, you may need more or less time.

5. Remove from the heat. Let cool 5 to 10 minutes before serving.

VARIATION: You don't need the bacon, but it adds flavor and keeps the corn from getting dry. For a vegetarian version, brush the corn with olive oil instead. In lieu of ranch seasoning, try lemon-pepper seasoning.

Fruity Trail Mix

PREP TIME: 10 minutes   YIELD: Serves 4

DAIRY-FREE, GLUTEN-FREE, NUT-FREE, SOY-FREE, VEGAN, 30 MINUTES OR LESS

Dried fruit is a delicious snack, but you may be surprised to learn that many dried fruits have added sugar. Be sure to check the label and purchase only unsweetened products if you want to control the amount of sugar. Some of the fruits, like mangos and pineapple, may need to be chopped into smaller pieces. Besides being a snack, this can be added to oatmeal or yogurt.

1 cup raisins

1 cup dried pineapple

1 cup dried bananas

1 cup dried apricots

1 cup dried mangos

1. In a medium bowl, combine the raisins, pineapple, bananas, apricots, and mangos.

2. Store in a plastic container or plastic bag.

VARIATION: You can use any fruit that you enjoy, such as apples, dates, cherries, peaches, blueberries, cranberries, or flaked coconut.

Fire-Roasted Artichokes

PREP TIME: 10 minutes   **COOK TIME:** 20 minutes   **YIELD:** Serves 4

GLUTEN-FREE, NUT-FREE, VEGETARIAN, 30 MINUTES OR LESS

A friend of mine introduced me to cooking artichokes over the fire. I love eating them with this dip.

4 artichokes

2 tablespoons olive oil

½ cup mayonnaise

3 tablespoons grated Parmesan

1 teaspoon garlic salt

1 tablespoon lemon juice

1. Drizzle the artichokes with the olive oil. Wrap each artichoke in a 16-inch piece of heavy-duty aluminum foil.

2. Gently place the wrapped artichokes on the coals. Cook for about 10 minutes, flip, then cook on the other side for 10 more minutes.

3. While the artichokes are cooking, in a small bowl, mix together the mayonnaise, Parmesan, garlic salt, and lemon juice until smooth. If it is too thick, add a little bit of water to desired consistency.

4. Remove the artichokes from the heat. Let sit for 5 minutes and serve hot with the dip.

COOKING TIP: You can cook these in the foil over the campfire on a grate, or you can cut them in half and grill them, unwrapped, over low heat.

Chocolate–Peanut Butter Energy Balls

PREP TIME: 5 minutes, plus 1 to 2 hours to chill   YIELD: Serves 4

SOY-FREE, VEGETARIAN

When I was a kid, my mom would buy huge jars of peanut butter. We would make this recipe often, just to use up the peanut butter. I discovered these make a good high-protein snack, even though they do soften in the heat. Rolling them in graham crackers helps them keep their shape.

1 cup chunky peanut butter

1 cup powdered milk or
   protein powder

½ cup honey

¼ cup mini chocolate chips

½ cup crushed graham crackers

1. In a medium bowl, combine the peanut butter, powdered milk, honey, and chocolate chips.

2. Put the crushed graham crackers in a separate bowl.

3. Using clean hands, roll the peanut butter mixture into marble-size balls.

4. Roll the balls in the crushed graham crackers and chill for 1 to 2 hours, or until firm.

5. Keep in an airtight container for up to 1 week.

Grilled Cheddar-Jalapeño Flatbread

PREP TIME: 10 minutes   **COOK TIME:** 10 minutes   **YIELD:** Serves 4

NUT-FREE, SOY-FREE, VEGETARIAN, 30 MINUTES OR LESS

This is one of my favorite snacks to eat when we're spending time together around the campfire and enjoying a drink. It is easy to make and pairs well with adult beverages. Think of it as bar food for camping.

½ teaspoon olive oil or cooking spray

1 (8-ounce) flatbread

¼ cup shredded cheddar cheese

¼ cup sliced jalapeños

1. Brush the olive oil on the flatbread.

2. Sprinkle the cheese on the flatbread and top with the jalapeños.

3. Cook the flatbread on a campfire grate over low heat until the cheese has melted and the bottom of the flatbread is crispy, 5 to 10 minutes.

4. Cut into pieces. Serve hot or warm.

VARIATION: This is pretty much a sauceless pizza. Try other flavors, such as cheddar and pepperoni, mozzarella and tomatoes, or feta and olives.

Seasoned Popcorn

PREP TIME: 5 minutes　　　**COOK TIME:** 10 minutes　　　**YIELD:** Serves 1

ONE-POT, GLUTEN-FREE, 30 MINUTES OR LESS

Popcorn is the snack you can make anywhere, backpacking or camping. And what makes this the perfect popcorn for camping is the special seasoning. This recipe is for making popcorn in a 1-liter backpacking pot.

1 teaspoon olive oil

3 tablespoons popcorn kernels

1 tablespoon butter powder

1 tablespoon gluten-free chicken
　bouillon powder

1 tablespoon brewer's yeast

PREP AHEAD

Mix together the butter powder, chicken bouillon powder, and brewer's yeast. Store the mixture in a saltshaker.

1. In a small pot on a camp stove, heat the oil for 2 to 3 minutes, then add the kernels and cover. Shake the pot so the kernels are evenly coated. It normally takes 5 to 6 minutes for all of the kernels to pop.

2. Once the popcorn stops popping, remove from the heat.

3. Wait 2 to 3 minutes before opening the lid so that any extra popping doesn't cause the popcorn to go everywhere.

4. Sprinkle with the butter powder, bouillon, and brewer's yeast. Enjoy.

VARIATION: You can buy seasonings for popcorn at most stores and online if you want other variations. I also like flavoring my popcorn with ranch dressing powder as an alternative.

COOKING TIP: If you are not backpacking, you can make this in a Dutch oven, a cast-iron skillet, or a regular pot. For 4 servings, use 2 tablespoons of olive oil and 1/3 cup of popcorn kernels and quadruple the amount of seasoning.

Israeli Pearled Couscous

PREP TIME: 5 minutes   **COOK TIME:** 20 minutes   **YIELD:** Serves 4

ONE-PAN, SOY-FREE, VEGAN, 30 MINUTES OR LESS

This is one of my favorite sides to make both at home and while camping. It goes well with any meat dish or even with a salad for a meatless dinner. Depending on the brand, it will be labeled as pearled or Israeli couscous and can be found in any grocery store.

1 tablespoon olive oil

1 cup pearled or Israeli couscous

2 cups water

2 tablespoons ketchup

1 teaspoon paprika

Salt

Black pepper

1. In a pan on a camp stove over medium heat, heat the olive oil. Once the oil is hot, add the couscous. Stir the couscous until it has been toasted to a golden brown.

2. Add the water, ketchup, and paprika, and bring to a boil over high heat.

3. Reduce the heat to medium and boil for 8 to 10 minutes, uncovered.

4. Stir well and cook, covered, for an additional 4 to 6 minutes, or until the couscous is soft and no water remains. Season with salt and pepper to taste, and enjoy.

Watermelon and Feta Plate

PREP TIME: 10 minutes   YIELD: Serves 4
GLUTEN-FREE, NUT-FREE, SOY-FREE, 30 MINUTES OR LESS

What is a camping trip without watermelon? It makes a delicious and healthy snack, and this twist adds something extra. Feta and watermelon are a very popular combination in Israel, especially at the beach restaurants. The saltiness of the feta goes perfectly with sweet watermelon.

1 (2-pound) watermelon   1 (8-ounce) block feta cheese

1. Cube the watermelon into bite-size pieces and cut the feta in half horizontally and then into thin slices. It's okay if the cheese crumbles a little bit.

2. Arrange the watermelon and feta on a plate or tray.

3. Serve immediately.

VARIATION: To make this into a salad, crumble the feta cheese, add 2 tablespoons of chopped fresh basil, and drizzle with 2 tablespoons of balsamic vinegar.

chocolate
chip cookies

marshmallow

milk
chocolate bar

BROOKIE'S S'MOOKIES

DESSERTS

Brookie's S'mookies

PREP TIME: 5 minutes   COOK TIME: 5 minutes   YIELD: Serves 4

NUT-FREE, SOY-FREE, 30 MINUTES OR LESS

After trying these, you may never use graham crackers for s'mores again. My oldest daughter, Brook, and her best friend came up with these one day using soft chocolate chip cookies. Switching out just one ingredient in an otherwise classic recipe makes the flavor and texture very different.

1 (1.4-ounce) chocolate bar   4 marshmallows

8 soft chocolate chip cookies

1. Break the chocolate bar into 4 pieces. Put 1 piece on top of each of the 4 cookies and set all 8 cookies near the fire, either on a rock or on a campfire grate away from direct heat, so the chocolate melts while you are roasting the marshmallows. Don't set them too close or the cookies will burn.

2. Using skewers, roast the marshmallows until golden brown, 30 to 40 seconds on each side, depending on how hot your fire is.

3. Once the marshmallows are roasted, sandwich them between the cookies. Enjoy while still warm and gooey.

Rocky Road S'more Roll-Ups

PREP TIME: 5 minutes   **COOK TIME:** 15 minutes   **YIELD:** Serves 4

VEGETARIAN, 30 MINUTES OR LESS

This is an interesting variation on a wrap that makes a great camping dessert. I use flour tortillas, but you can also use store-bought crepes or pancakes. These can also be eaten cold if there are fire restrictions.

2 tablespoons olive oil or
  cooking spray

4 flour tortillas

8 tablespoons Nutella or other
  chocolate-hazelnut spread

½ cup sliced almonds

1 cup mini marshmallows

1. Tear 4 (12-inch) pieces of heavy-duty aluminum foil. Grease them lightly with the olive oil.

2. Spread each tortilla with Nutella. Sprinkle the almonds and marshmallows on top.

3. Roll up each tortilla and wrap it in a piece of the prepared foil.

4. Gently lay the packets over the coals. Cook for 5 to 7 minutes, flip the packets, then cook for 5 to 7 minutes more, or until warm.

5. Serve warm.

Donut S'mores

PREP TIME: 5 minutes   **COOK TIME:** 5 minutes   **YIELD:** Serves 4

SOY-FREE, NUT-FREE, 30 MINUTES OR LESS

I often grab a box of donuts at the store for breakfast or a snack before we head out camping. I make sure to save some of the glazed ones to make this recipe. Fresh donuts are fine, but day-old ones work well, too. If you have access to them, try this recipe with Krispy Kreme doughnuts.

1 (1.4-ounce) milk chocolate bar   4 glazed donuts

4 marshmallows

1. Break the chocolate bar into 4 quarters and each quarter into 3 or 4 smaller pieces. Set aside.

2. Place 1 marshmallow into the hole of each donut. Skewer the donuts.

3. Lightly toast one side of each donut over the fire for 30 to 60 seconds and remove from the heat.

4. Flip the donuts and place one-quarter of the chocolate pieces on the toasted side. Return to the heat, toasting the other side until the chocolate is melted, 30 to 60 seconds. You might need more time, depending on the heat of the fire.

5. Remove from the heat and serve warm.

INGREDIENT TIP: Many bakeries and stores have gluten-free donuts that can be used for this recipe if gluten is a concern.

SERVING TIP: Try these in the morning with a cup of coffee or hot cocoa.

Fire Season S'mores

PREP TIME: 5 minutes   **YIELD:** Serves 4
30 MINUTES OR LESS

The height of fire season typically hits around the first week of August, and then fires and even gas grills are prohibited. This has all the flavors of a s'more without the need for a campfire. Nutella can be found online or in the same aisle as the peanut butter in the grocery store.

4 graham cracker sheets

4 tablespoons Nutella or other
  chocolate-hazelnut spread

4 tablespoons marshmallow fluff

1. Break each graham cracker sheet in half.

2. Spread one half with Nutella. On the other half, spread the marshmallow fluff.

3. Sandwich the halves together and enjoy.

VARIATION: Try adding strawberry or banana slices for additional flavor. You can also try chocolate and peanut butter, too.

Caramel-Apple S'Mores

PREP TIME: 5 minutes   **COOK TIME:** 5 minutes   **YIELD:** Serves 4

GLUTEN-FREE, NUT-FREE, SOY-FREE, 30 MINUTES OR LESS

This was an accidental recipe that has now become a family tradition. During one camping trip, I forgot the graham crackers at home. What was I going to do? (Because you know camping isn't the same without s'mores.) I sliced some apples and used those instead. The crunch and sweetness from the apple elevate s'mores to a whole new level.

1 large apple   4 soft caramel candies

4 marshmallows

1.   Core the apple and cut it into 8 even slices. Set them aside.

2.   Toast the marshmallows on skewers over the fire until they are golden brown, 30 to 40 seconds each side, depending on how hot your fire is.

3.   For each s'more, sandwich a marshmallow and a caramel candy between 2 apple slices. Enjoy.

VARIATION: If you do not have caramels, try caramel ice cream topping instead.

INGREDIENT TIP: If the caramels aren't soft enough, you can warm them near the fire so they soften more.

Chocolate-Orange Brownies

PREP TIME: 25 minutes   **COOK TIME:** 30 minutes   **YIELD:** Serves 4

DAIRY-FREE, NUT-FREE, SOY-FREE, VEGETARIAN

If you have never made these before, you are in for a treat. This decadent dessert is one of my favorites. It reminds me of the chocolate-covered orange peel candy you can find at Christmas. With this recipe, you can enjoy it throughout the year.

4 medium-to-large oranges

2 tablespoons olive oil or
  cooking spray

1 (18.2-ounce) package dark chocolate
  brownie mix

1 or 2 eggs as needed for the
  brownie mix

Water as needed for the brownie mix

Oil as needed for the brownie mix

PREP AHEAD

You can hollow out the oranges at home. Store the orange "cups" and their tops in an airtight container in the cooler until ready to use. The inside of the oranges can be used for Creamy Fruit Salad (page 60) or a cocktail.

1. Cut the tops from the oranges about ½ inch down. Using a spoon or butter knife, hollow out each orange, reserving the top.

2. Tear 4 (18-inch) pieces of heavy-duty aluminum foil. Grease them lightly with the olive oil.

3. Prepare the brownie mix with the eggs, water, and oil according to the package instructions.

4. Pour the brownie mix evenly into the hollowed-out oranges. Place the tops on the oranges.

5. Carefully wrap each orange tightly with a piece of the prepared foil.

6. Place the foil-wrapped oranges gently onto the coals. Cook for 10 to 15 minutes, flip them, then cook for 10 to 15 minutes more, or until the brownie is cooked through (the brownies are done when you stick a knife or toothpick in the center and it comes out clean). This may take more or less time depending on how hot your fire is.

7. Remove from the heat and let cool for 5 to 10 minutes. Open a foil packet and eat the brownie out of the orange with a spoon.

VARIATION: If you don't like dark chocolate, instead use milk chocolate brownie mix. For an alternative, you can also use a spice cake mix or a blueberry muffin mix.

Fire-Roasted Apples

PREP TIME: 10 minutes   **COOK TIME:** 20 minutes   **YIELD:** Serves 4

GLUTEN-FREE, SOY-FREE, VEGETARIAN, 30 MINUTES OR LESS

Fire-Roasted Apples are a classic family favorite. We especially enjoy these on our fall camping trips, the same time that farmers start selling apples in the farm stands. We live in an area that has many apple orchards, some of which are more than 100 years old. I especially like making these with local apples because it helps support the small businesses in our region.

3 tablespoons chopped walnuts

1 tablespoon maple syrup

3 tablespoons salted butter, at room temperature

½ teaspoon pumpkin pie spice

4 tart apples (such as Pink Lady, Jonathan, or McIntosh), cored but left intact

1. Tear 4 (12-inch) pieces of aluminum foil.

2. In a medium bowl, stir together the walnuts, maple syrup, butter, and pumpkin pie spice.

3. Fill the center of each apple with the mixture, then wrap each apple tightly in a piece of aluminum foil.

4. Gently place the apples over the coals. Cook for 8 to 10 minutes, flip them, then cook for 8 to 10 minutes more, or until the apples are cooked through.

5. Remove from the heat and let cool for 5 to 10 minutes. Carefully unwrap and enjoy.

VARIATION: Raisins or cranberries can also be added or substituted for the nuts for additional flavor. Try serving with ice cream or whipped topping.

COOKING TIP: These can also be made at home in the oven. Place the filled apples in a glass baking dish and bake at 375°F for 30 to 40 minutes.

Pineapple Upside-Down Cake Packets

PREP TIME: 10 minutes   **COOK TIME:** 15 minutes   **YIELD:** Serves 4

NUT-FREE, SOY-FREE, VEGETARIAN, 30 MINUTES OR LESS

Pineapple upside-down cake is one of my favorite desserts. I love this version, which makes a nice dessert for a birthday or other special occasion. I know that it seems like there is a lot of sugar, but if you use less, you won't get that caramelly, buttery "crust."

1 (11-ounce) prepared angel food cake

12 tablespoons salted butter, cubed

12 tablespoons light brown sugar

1 (20-ounce) can pineapple chunks or rings, drained

1 (10-ounce) jar maraschino cherries, drained

PREP AHEAD

You can slice the angel food cake at home. Store in an airtight container until you are ready to use.

1.   Tear 4 (16-inch) pieces of heavy-duty aluminum foil.

2.   Cut the angel food cake into 8 equal slices. On one half of each piece of foil, place 2 slices of angel food cake so they are overlapping.

3. For each cake, add on top, in the following order, 3 tablespoons butter, 3 tablespoons brown sugar, one-quarter of the pineapple, and one-quarter of the cherries.

4. Fold the other half of the foil over the cake, making sure that the edges are tightly sealed.

5. Gently place the foil packets on the coals, cherries-side down.

6. Cook for 8 to 10 minutes, then flip over and cook for 2 more minutes.

7. Remove from the heat. Carefully unwrap the foil and serve hot or warm.

VARIATION: You can also make this in a Dutch oven by layering the cherries on the bottom first. Use a well-seasoned Dutch oven or grease the bottom.

Butterscotch Monkey Bread

PREP TIME: 15 minutes   COOK TIME: 30 minutes   YIELD: Serves 4

NUT-FREE, SOY-FREE, VEGETARIAN

Monkey bread is a very traditional camping recipe, but this version includes butterscotch pudding, which makes it heavenly (and extra gooey). If you don't want to use a Dutch oven, you can make it in individual aluminum foil packets. If you are cooking for a crowd, this recipe can easily be doubled.

1 (16-ounce) tube jumbo biscuits

8 tablespoons (1 stick) salted butter

1 (3.5-ounce) package butterscotch pudding mix

1½ cups light brown sugar

1 tablespoon cinnamon

PREP AHEAD

You can mix together the pudding mix, brown sugar, and cinnamon at home. Store in a jar or airtight container until you are ready to use it.

1. Line a Dutch oven with parchment paper.

2. Cut each biscuit into 6 pieces. Set aside.

3. In a pan on a camp stove over low heat, melt the butter.

4. Gently place the biscuit dough in a zip-top bag or a container with a lid. Pour the butter over the dough to coat.

5. Add the butterscotch pudding mix, brown sugar, and cinnamon to the bag or container and shake until the dough is covered.

6. Transfer the contents to the prepared Dutch oven (including whatever is left in the bag).

7. Place the Dutch oven on the coals over medium heat. Cook for 25 to 30 minutes, rotating every 5 to 10 minutes, or until the dough is cooked through.

8. Serve hot or warm.

VARIATION: For more flavor, try adding chopped pecans or shredded coconut.

Pie-Iron Pies

PREP TIME: 10 minutes   **COOK TIME:** 20 minutes   **YIELD:** Serves 4

DAIRY-FREE, NUT-FREE, SOY-FREE, VEGAN, 30 MINUTES OR LESS

Most pie-iron recipes use bread or dough. For this version, I use bread because it is quicker, but you can also use store-bought pie dough; it just takes about 20 minutes longer, depending on how hot your fire is. Use 4 pie irons to cook all 4 pies at the same time.

2 to 3 tablespoons salted butter, at room temperature

8 slices white bread

8 tablespoons pie filling or jam, such as apple or cherry

3 tablespoons confectioners' sugar

1. For each pie, butter 2 slices of bread on one side. Place 1 slice of bread in a pie iron, buttered-side down, then add 2 tablespoons of pie filling.

2. Top with the second slice of bread, buttered-side up, and close the pie iron.

3. Cook for 8 to 10 minutes on each side, or until both sides are toasted.

4. Remove from the heat and let cool for 5 to 10 minutes. Remove from the pie iron, sprinkle with confectioners' sugar, and eat hot or warm.

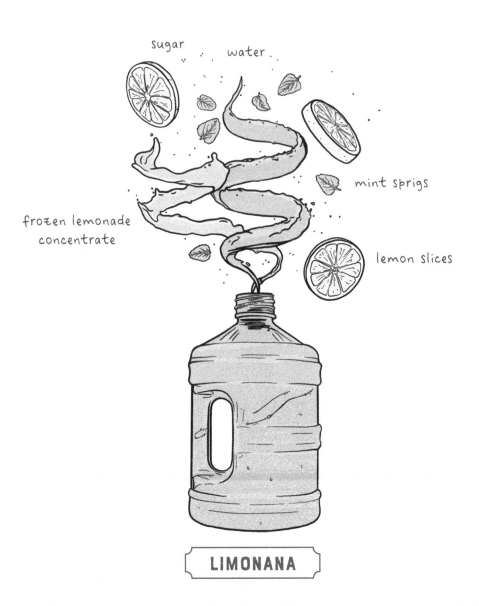

sugar

water

mint sprigs

frozen lemonade concentrate

lemon slices

LIMONANA

DRINKS

Homemade Hot Cocoa

PREP TIME: 5 minutes   **COOK TIME:** 10 minutes   **YIELD:** Serves 5

GLUTEN-FREE, NUT-FREE, SOY-FREE, VEGETARIAN, 30 MINUTES OR LESS

Hot cocoa is something that most people take with them camping. I prefer to use my own mix rather than a store-bought one. The cayenne and cinnamon are optional, but they really add depth. This recipe makes enough mix for 5 cups of hot cocoa.

1 cup confectioners' sugar

½ cup unsweetened cocoa powder

1 cup powdered milk

2 teaspoons ground cinnamon (optional)

1 teaspoon ground cayenne pepper (optional)

5 cups water

PREP AHEAD

At home, sift together the sugar, cocoa powder, powdered milk, cinnamon (if using), and cayenne pepper (if using). Store in an airtight container or a 1-pint mason jar. This mix can keep for up to 6 months.

1. Mix the confectioners' sugar, cocoa powder, powdered milk, cinnamon (if using), and cayenne (if using) together in a container.

2. Over the campfire or on a camp stove, bring 1 cup of water to a boil for each serving of hot cocoa.

3. Scoop ½ cup of hot cocoa mix into a cup for each serving.

4. Add the boiling water and stir well.

5. Serve hot or warm.

VARIATION: If you like your hot cocoa boozy, try adding a splash or a shot of any of the following: bourbon, peppermint schnapps, coffee liqueur, scotch, or Irish cream. You can also add 1 cup of mini marshmallows to the mix.

Spiced Apple Cider

PREP TIME: 10 minutes   **COOK TIME:** 40 minutes to 3 hours   **YIELD:** Serves 4

ONE-PAN, DAIRY-FREE, GLUTEN-FREE, NUT-FREE, SOY-FREE, VEGAN

This makes the perfect hot drink for those nights camping in the fall. If you do not have a lot of time or fuel at the campsite, make this at home on the stove instead, and heat it up when you are camping.

2 quarts apple cider

12 green cardamom pods, gently crushed, or 4 teaspoons cardamom seeds, gently crushed

4 star anise pods

2 tablespoons pumpkin pie spice

Cinnamon sticks, for serving (optional)

PREP AHEAD

At home, mix together the cardamom, star anise, and pumpkin pie spice. Store in an airtight container or glass jar until ready to use.

1. In a pot over the fire or on a camp stove over low heat, combine the apple cider, cardamom, star anise, and pumpkin pie spice. Cook for 5 to 10 minutes, or until the mixture starts to simmer.

2. Continue to simmer for 30 minutes or up to 3 hours, stirring occasionally.

3. Remove from the heat and serve hot with a cinnamon stick (if using).

Bonfire Shandy

PREP TIME: 5 minutes   **YIELD:** Serves 2

DAIRY-FREE, NUT-FREE, SOY-FREE, VEGAN, 30 MINUTES OR LESS

This is the perfect drink to enjoy by the bonfire—it's one of my favorites. It is light and sweet and meant to share. Shandy is often made with lemonade, but I think you'll like the extra fizz you get with soda. I like to make this with 7UP, but you can use any lemon-lime soda.

1 (12-ounce) can beer, chilled

1 (12-ounce) can lemon-lime
 soda, chilled

4 maraschino cherries

2 slices lemon

1. Pour the beer evenly into 2 glasses.

2. Gently pour the soda into the beer in equal parts.

3. Stir with a spoon or straw (if you have it) and garnish each with 2 cherries and 1 lemon slice.

INGREDIENT TIP: To keep your drinks cool while camping, store your glasses inside the cooler until you are ready to pour a drink.

Chai Tea

PREP TIME: 10 minutes   **COOK TIME:** 10 minutes   **YIELD:** 5 servings

ONE-POT, DAIRY-FREE, GLUTEN-FREE, NUT-FREE, SOY-FREE, VEGAN, 30 MINUTES OR LESS

I love chai tea and drink it most mornings even when I am not camping because although I like caffeine, coffee can be harsh. There is something about making this over a camp stove or campfire early in the morning that makes it even better. Traditional chai is sometimes made with black peppercorns as well; you can choose to add 1 tablespoon of whole black peppercorns to this if you like.

5 cups water

1 cinnamon stick

8 cardamom pods or 3 teaspoons
   cardamom seeds

4 whole cloves

5 teaspoons powdered ginger or
   2 inches fresh ginger, thinly sliced
   or grated

4 tablespoons loose-leaf black tea

Maple syrup or sugar (optional)

PREP AHEAD

You can make the chai mix at home. Use a mortar and pestle or the bottom of a heavy pan to lightly crush the cinnamon stick, cardamom pods, and cloves. Transfer to an airtight container or glass jar and add the powdered ginger and loose-leaf tea. This mix will last up to 6 months.

1. In a pot on a camp stove over low heat, bring 1 cup of water per serving to a simmer.

2. Using a heavy pan, lightly crush the cinnamon stick, cardamom pods, and cloves and put them in a small bowl. Add the ginger and tea and mix well.

3. For each serving, add 1 heaping tablespoon of the spiced tea mixture to the water and simmer for 1 to 2 minutes.

4. Stir well and remove from the heat. Let sit for 2 minutes, then strain out the spices.

5. Sweeten with maple syrup if desired and serve hot (see Variation).

VARIATION: You can make this with milk, half-and-half, or heavy (whipping) cream by substituting any of these for half of the water. You can also use bags of black tea instead of loose-leaf tea.

SERVING TIP: Use a tea strainer if you have one, so all you have to do is remove it once the tea has brewed.

Peanut Butter & Jelly Cocktail

PREP TIME: 5 minutes   YIELD: Serves 1
GLUTEN-FREE, SOY-FREE, VEGETARIAN, 30 MINUTES OR LESS

Have you ever had a peanut butter and jelly drink? For this cocktail, I like to use huckleberry sweet cream liqueur made in Montana by Willie's Distillery and Screwball peanut butter whiskey. But you can use any nut-flavored liqueur and any berry-flavored liqueur. If I don't have ice, I keep everything in the cooler and as cold as possible before serving.

1 (1.5-ounce) shot peanut butter whiskey or nut-flavored liqueur

1 (1.5-ounce) shot berry-flavored liqueur

½ cup heavy (whipping) cream, half-and-half, or milk

1. Pour the peanut butter whiskey, berry liqueur, and heavy cream into a jar or shaker, with ice if you have it.

2. Shake the contents for 1 to 2 minutes.

3. Pour into a cup and enjoy.

BACKPACKING TIP: To adapt this for backpacking, replace the milk with 1 cup of water and 2 tablespoons of powdered milk. Make sure that the powdered milk is completely dissolved in the water.

Limonana

PREP TIME: 10 minutes   YIELD: Serves 4

DAIRY-FREE, GLUTEN-FREE, NUT-FREE, SOY-FREE, VEGAN, 30 MINUTES OR LESS

This is one of the most refreshing drinks I have ever tasted. *Nana* is the Hebrew word for "mint" and *limon* is the Hebrew word for "lemon." You can often find this drink at any beach restaurant in Israel. It's the perfect drink for when you need to quench your thirst. It's best served over ice, but drinking it cold out of the cooler is just as good.

5 mint sprigs

1 (12-ounce) can frozen
   lemonade concentrate

6 cups water

Lemon slices (optional)

2 tablespoons sugar (optional)

1. Remove the mint leaves from the stems. Chop the mint leaves as finely as you can.

2. In a 1-gallon pitcher, mix together the lemonade concentrate, water, and mint.

3. Add ice if you have it, and add the lemon slices (if using) and sugar (if using).

VARIATION: Make this into a cocktail by adding a splash or a shot of any of the following: tequila, lemon vodka, or anise liquor.

Backpacker's Cocktail

PREP TIME: 5 minutes   YIELD: Serves 1

DAIRY-FREE, GLUTEN-FREE, NUT-FREE, SOY-FREE, VEGAN, 30 MINUTES OR LESS

It's not always easy to find something delicious to drink when you are way out in the backcountry. You have to think about the weight of items and about keeping things cold. This little cocktail is what we take with us when we back-pack and want a nice alcoholic beverage at the end of the day. It is definitely more portable than beer or a box of wine.

1 (1.09-ounce) package instant lemonade mix

1 (1.5-ounce) shot vodka

10 freeze-dried blueberries

Pinch sugar

1 cup water

1. In a cup, mix together the lemonade mix, vodka, blueberries, and sugar. Let sit for 5 minutes.

2. Add the water and stir thoroughly.

3. Enjoy.

INGREDIENT TIP: One of the best ways to keep alcohol cold while back-packing is to store it in a bottle in a cold lake or stream. Be sure it sinks and doesn't float away.

Fruity Wine Spritzer

PREP TIME: 10 minutes   **YIELD:** Serves 4

DAIRY-FREE, GLUTEN-FREE, NUT-FREE, SOY-FREE, VEGAN

If you use a lot of fruit when you go camping, here is one of the ways you can use up any extras, like leftover watermelon from Creamy Fruit Salad (page 60) or the orange pieces from Chocolate-Orange Brownies (page 148). If you don't have ice on hand, try using frozen fruit instead.

2 (12-ounce) cans flavored soda water (such as citrus- or berry-flavored)

1 cup chopped strawberries

1 cup chopped watermelon

1 cup chopped oranges

3 cups red dessert wine

1. In a 1-gallon pitcher, mix the soda water, strawberries, watermelon, oranges, and red dessert wine.

2. Add ice if you have it, or chill in the cooler before drinking.

VARIATION: If you do not have a dessert wine, use 3 cups of regular wine instead and add simple syrup. To make a basic simple syrup, heat ½ cup of water and ½ cup of sugar in a pan until all the sugar is dissolved. Add the syrup to the wine a little at a time until it reaches your desired sweetness.

MEASUREMENT CONVERSIONS

OVEN TEMPERATURES

FAHRENHEIT	CELSIUS (APPROXIMATE)
250°F	120°C
300°F	150°C
325°F	165°C
350°F	180°C
375°F	190°C
400°F	200°C
425°F	220°C
450°F	230°C

WEIGHT EQUIVALENTS

U.S. STANDARD	METRIC (APPROXIMATE)
½ ounce	15 g
1 ounce	30 g
2 ounces	60 g
4 ounces	115 g
8 ounces	225 g
12 ounces	340 g
16 ounces or 1 pound	455 g

VOLUME EQUIVALENTS

	U.S. STANDARD	U.S. STANDARD (OUNCES)	METRIC (APPROXIMATE)
LIQUID	2 tablespoons	1 fl. oz.	30 mL
	¼ cup	2 fl. oz.	60 mL
	½ cup	4 fl. oz.	120 mL
	1 cup	8 fl. oz.	240 mL
	1½ cups	12 fl. oz.	355 mL
	2 cups or 1 pint	16 fl. oz.	475 mL
	4 cups or 1 quart	32 fl. oz.	1 L
	1 gallon	128 fl. oz.	4 L
DRY	⅛ teaspoon	—	0.5 mL
	¼ teaspoon	—	1 mL
	½ teaspoon	—	2 mL
	¾ teaspoon	—	4 mL
	1 teaspoon	—	5 mL
	1 tablespoon	—	15 mL
	¼ cup	—	59 mL
	⅓ cup	—	79 mL
	½ cup	—	118 mL
	⅔ cup	—	156 mL
	¾ cup	—	177 mL
	1 cup	—	235 mL
	2 cups or 1 pint	—	475 mL
	3 cups	—	700 mL
	4 cups or 1 quart	—	1 L
	½ gallon	—	2 L
	1 gallon	—	4 L

RESOURCES

Alpine Touch

AlpineTouch.com

For more than 50 years, this Montana-based spice company has been selling an all-purpose blend that's perfect for camp cooking. Alpine also makes meat rubs, lemon-pepper seasoning, and seasoned salt.

Coleman

Coleman.com

The website for outdoor gear manufacturer Coleman is where you can find some of the best coolers and camp stoves, as well as other camping gear, like tents and sleeping bags.

Lodge

LodgeCastIron.com

Lodge is one of the most trusted and popular brands for cast-iron cookware. Besides cast-iron cookware, it is an excellent source for cast-iron tips and care.

Mama Bear Outdoors

MamaBearOutdoors.com

Mama Bear Outdoors is an online resource for everything outdoors, including tips and gear recommendations for camping, backpacking, hiking, fishing, and other outdoor adventures.

MontYBoca

MontYBoca.com

A camp cooking resource from a professionally trained chef and lifelong adventurer, Chef Corso. You will find community-tested camping and backpacking recipes, meal plans, cookbooks, and tips for camp cooking.

Pull Start Fire

PullStartFire.com

Pull Start's fire starter will get you cooking in no time. It requires no matches or lighter and will quickly start your fire within minutes.

UCO

UCOGear.com

UCO has many camping accessories, like sporks, lanterns, headlamps, and mess kits. It is one of the best places to find all your little camping tools.

INDEX

Acknowledgments

Once again, I am so thankful that Callisto Media gave me another opportunity to write a cookbook. Special thanks to Joe Cho for reaching out and to my awesome editor, Anne Lowrey, as well as all the other amazing people that were involved with this book.

A huge shout-out to my husband and kids for being so patient with me and supportive during this crazy process. They did it before and they did it again with very little complaining. They make the best taste testers and helpers while cooking.

A huge thank-you to the rest of my family and friends who provided feedback and were great taste testers. I am so grateful to all of those who inspire me, including my 15 siblings, my parents, and Sheldon and Vickie. This time, many of the recipes in this cookbook were inspired by all of my "family" from Hadasim. My awesome sisters-in-law, Amber and Liz, gave amazing feedback and suggestions yet again. I don't want to forget my "bonus" children, Lindsey and Kayden, who make my life fuller and are always ready to go camping with my family. And finally, I am grateful for my amazing readers who keep coming back for more.

About the Author

 **Pauline Reynolds-Nuttall** lives on a mountain in the gorgeous Bitterroot Mountains in Montana with her husband, three children, two dogs, chickens, and the occasional black bear or mountain lion. She was raised in both Montana and Israel but is finally back home in the mountains and gullies of her childhood. During the day, Pauline works in human services helping others, and at night, she writes about her love for the outdoors. She loves fishing, hiking, backpacking, and camping. This is her second cookbook; she previously wrote *Cast-Iron Camping Cookbook*. You can find her online at MamaBearOutdoors.com and on Facebook, Twitter, Instagram, and Pinterest @MamaBearOutdoors.

CPSIA information can be obtained
at www.ICGtesting.com
Printed in the USA
JSHW011912171021
19623JS00001B/1

9 781648 763915